TECHNOLOGY AND SOCIETY

TECHNOLOGY AND SOCIETY

Advisory Editor
DANIEL J. BOORSTIN, author of
The Americans and Director of
The National Museum of History
and Technology, Smithsonian Institution

INDUSTRIAL RESEARCH

IN THE

UNITED STATES OF AMERICA

BY

A. P. M. FLEMING

ARNO PRESS
A NEW YORK TIMES COMPANY
New York • 1972

Reprint Edition 1972 by Arno Press Inc.

Reprinted from a copy in The University of
Illinois Library

Technology and Society
ISBN for complete set: 0-405-04680-4
See last pages of this volume for titles.

Manufactured in the United States of America

Library of Congress Cataloging in Publication Data

   Fleming, Sir Arthur Percy Morris, 1881-1960.
      Industrial research in the United States of America.

    (Technology and society)
    Reprint of the 1917 ed., which was issued as no. 1
in series: Gt. Brit. Privy Council. Committee for
Scientific and Industrial Research. Science and
industry.
    1. Research, Industrial. 2. Technical education
--United States. I. Title. II. Series. III. Se-
ries: Great Britain. Privy Council. Committee for
Scientific and Industrial Research. Science and
industry, no. 1.
T176.F48   1972   607'.2'73   72-5050
ISBN 0-405-04702-9

SCIENCE AND INDUSTRY

A SERIES OF PAPERS BEARING
ON INDUSTRIAL RESEARCH

Number One

INDUSTRIAL RESEARCH

IN THE

UNITED STATES OF AMERICA

BY

A. P. M. FLEMING, M.I.E.E.

LONDON:
Published for the Department of Scientific and Industrial Research
by His Majesty's Stationery Office.

1917.

PREFACE.

This paper is the first of a series which the Advisory Council for Scientific and Industrial Research intend to issue, as announced in their first annual report.* But for the war the series would already have included several numbers. As it is Mr. Fleming's description of the industrial research being undertaken by the great related nation in America must suffice as some indication of the kind of information which it is hoped that "Science and Industry" will supply when the return of peace enables us to carry out our original plans.

Lord Milner has emphasised the necessity this country is under of readjusting its sense of "scale" in dealing with the problems of industry and among them research.† Nothing is more likely to help us to do this than a realisation of the progress already made in the United States as described and illustrated in the following pages. It is not to be imagined that all American industry has reached these standards ; far from it. Dr. Whitney, the Director of the research laboratories of the General Electric Company, in an address‡ delivered recently, deplored the neglect of true scientific research in the Universities and Colleges of the United States, and pointed out how essential research in pure science always is to industrial advance. The number of firms in the United States which have learnt the value of scientific research, in the sense of that term as it is used by Dr. Whitney and applied by the General Electric Company, is still limited. But the example is contagious, and manufacturers in this country cannot safely rely upon the instances here described remaining isolated. It is certain that they will not.

Mr. Fleming's report was prepared for publication in this series by the courtesy of the Directors of the British Westinghouse Electric and Manufacturing Company as the result of a visit to the United States which he made last year, and which he was allowed by his Directors to extend for the purposes of this report. The Advisory Council for Scientific and Industrial Research desire to take this opportunity of thanking the British Westinghouse Company and Mr. Fleming for the valuable contribution they have thus made to the cause of British industrial efficiency.

Mr. Fleming discusses in the closing sections of his paper a number of fundamental questions which his experiences have raised in his own mind and which his readers will be no less likely to ask. To some of them he suggests answers which cannot fail

---

* Report of the Committee of the Privy Council for Scientific and Industrial Research, 1915-16 (Cd. 8336), p. 29.
† Introduction to " The Elements of Reconstruction," Nisbet & Co., Ltd.
‡ Reported in " The Engineer," March 16, 1917, pp. 245-6.

to stimulate thought and discussion. If they have this effect one of the principal purposes of the author will have been served. The Advisory Council reserve their own judgment upon his proposals for further consideration in the light of the experience which is being gathered day by day.

May 1917.

DEPARTMENT OF SCIENTIFIC AND INDUSTRIAL RESEARCH,
GREAT GEORGE STREET, WESTMINSTER, S.W. 1.

TABLE OF CONTENTS.

	Page
INTRODUCTION.—Industrial Research—Pure Science Research	1
(I) CLASSIFICATION OF INDUSTRIAL RESEARCH LABORATORIES	2
(II) MANUFACTURING CORPORATIONS—Nature of research work carried out—(a) Research applied to elimination of manufacturing troubles—(b) Research having specific commercial object—(c) Research in pure science—(d) Research applied to public service—(e) Research in connection with standards for purchasing raw materials	2
(III) EXAMPLES OF INDUSTRIAL RESEARCH LABORATORIES OF MANUFACTURING CORPORATIONS	4
American Rolling Mill Company	4
American Brass Company	5
Detroit Edison Company	5
Dodge Brothers	6
Du Pont de Nemours & Company	6
Eastman Kodak Company	7
General Electric Company	8
General Motors Company	10
The B.F. Goodrich Company	10
International Acheson Graphite Company	11
National Carbon Company	11
National Cash Register Company	12
National Electric Lamp Association	13
New Jersey Zinc Company	14
Pennsylvania Railroad Company	15
Reo Motor Company	16
Studebaker Corporation	16
T. A. Edison Laboratories	17
Westinghouse Electric and Manufacturing Company	17
Western Electric Company	18
Other Companies	18
Résumé of principal features of the research of manufacturing corporations	19
(IV) ASSOCIATIONS OF MANUFACTURERS	20
National Canners' Association Laboratories	20
(V) UNIVERSITIES AND COLLEGES—(a) Graduating theses by students—(b) Pure science research by staff—(c) Research by staff for private firms—(d) Research in Experiment Stations	21
(VI) EXAMPLES OF UNIVERSITY RESEARCH	22
Clark University	22
Columbia University	23
Cornell University	23
Harvard University	24
Illinois State University	24
Iowa State College	26
Kansas University	26
Lehigh University	27
Michigan University	27
Ohio State University	28

	Page.
(VI) EXAMPLES OF UNIVERSITY RESEARCH—*continued*.	
Princeton University	28
Worcester Polytechnic Institute	28
Land Grant Colleges	28
Other Colleges	28
(VII) THE MELLON INSTITUTE OF INDUSTRIAL RESEARCH	29
(VIII) NATIONAL INSTITUTIONS	31
Bureau of Standards	32
Carnegie Institution	34
Smithsonian Institution	35
Department of Agriculture	35
Forest Products Laboratory	36
Bureau of Mines	37
(IX) COMMERCIAL RESEARCH LABORATORIES	39
Institute of Industrial Research, Washington	39
Electrical Testing Laboratories, New York	39
The Fitzgerald Laboratories, Inc., Niagara Falls	40
Detroit Testing Laboratories	40
Pittsburg Testing Laboratory	40
Laboratory of A. D. Little, Inc., Boston, Mass.	41
Wahl-Henius Institute of Fermentology, Chicago	42
(X) SCIENTIFIC SOCIETIES	42
(XI) ENDOWMENTS FOR SCIENTIFIC RESEARCH	43
(XII) CO-ORDINATION OF RESEARCH IN THE UNITED STATES—Movements towards nationalisation of research—Newlands Bill—American Association for Advancement of Science—Franklin Institute—Naval Advisory Board—Department of Agriculture and Bureau of Mines research organisation	44
(XIII) SELECTION AND TRAINING OF RESEARCH MEN	46
(XIV) FUNDAMENTAL CONSIDERATIONS IN INDUSTRIAL RESEARCH—Neglect of application of research—Relation to International Markets—Co-ordination of scientific resources and contemporary research—Collection and distribution of scientific data—Scientific discovery in relation to public benefit—Research in relation to the capitalist, the manufacturer, and the educationist	48
(XV) ORGANISATION OF BRITISH INDUSTRIAL RESEARCH—Inadequacy of present organisation—Necessity for organisation on national lines—Imperial research organisation—Financial aspect—Possible schemes for Great Britain—(*a*) Individual works laboratories—(*b*) Laboratories for a group of works in the same industry—(*c*) Centralisation of research in universities and colleges—(*d*) Centralised Imperial Research Laboratory for whole of industry	50
(XVI) CONCLUSIONS	55
INDEX	57

LIST OF ILLUSTRATIONS.

Plate.

AMERICAN ROLLING MILL COMPANY:—

1. Research Building.
2. Magnetic Laboratory.
3. Photomicrographic Laboratory.

AMERICAN BRASS COMPANY:—

4. Physical and Electrical Laboratory, Ansonia.
5. Electrolytic Laboratory, Waterbury.

EASTMAN KODAK COMPANY:—

6. Research Building.
7. Plant for Plate Manufacture.
8. Spectrophotometer.
9. Automatic Sensitometer Control.
10. Large Projection Room.
11. Research Work in Developers.
12. Photographic Laboratory.
13. Physico-Chemical Laboratory.
14. Laboratory for Colloidal Chemistry.
15. Organic Laboratory.

GENERAL ELECTRIC COMPANY:—

16. Research Building.
17. Laboratory for Insulation Research.
18. Laboratory for Magnetic Research.
19. Furnace Room.
20. Laboratory for Coolidge X-Ray Tubes.
21. Tungsten Reduction Furnaces.

NATIONAL CASH REGISTER COMPANY:—

22. Register Testing Machine.

NATIONAL ELECTRIC LAMP ASSOCIATION:—

23. General View of Laboratories and Park.
24. Engineering Building.
25. Physical Laboratory.
26. Interior of Physical Laboratory.

Plate.

PENNSYLVANIA RAILROAD COMPANY:—

27. General View of Laboratory Building.
28. Locomotive Testing Laboratory.
29. Spring Testing Laboratory.
30. Physical Laboratory.
31. Heat Treatment Laboratory.
32. Electrical Laboratory for Photometry.
33. Lamp Testing Laboratory.
34. Heat Insulation Laboratory.
35. General Chemical Laboratory.
36. Laboratory Car.
37. Dynamometer Car.
38. Brake Shoe Testing Laboratory.

REO MOTOR CAR COMPANY:—

39. Experimental Motor Testing Laboratory.

T. A. EDISON LABORATORIES:—

40. Chemical Laboratory.
41. Interior of Chemical Laboratory.

WESTINGHOUSE ELECTRIC AND MANUFACTURING COMPANY:—

42. Chemical Laboratory.
43. Physical Laboratory.
44. Magnetic Laboratory.
45. High Tension Laboratory.
46. Moulded Insulation Laboratory.
47. Vapour Converter Research employing Works Equipment.
48. Flywheel Investigations in works.
49. New Research Building in course of construction.

WESTERN ELECTRIC COMPANY:—

50. Circuit Laboratory.
51. Telephone Instrument Laboratory.
52. Transmission Branch Laboratory.

Plate.
UNIVERSITY OF ILLINOIS:—

53. Railway Dynamometer Car.
54. Interior of Dynamometer Car.
55. Locomotive Testing Laboratory.
56. Electric Test Car.
57. Apparatus for Special Research.
58. Apparatus for Special Magnetic Research.
59. Air Washing Plant.
60. Electric Dynamometer developed for Research.
61. Dynamometer Investigations on Machine Tools.

WORCESTER POLYTECHNIC INSTITUTE:—

62. Electric Test Car, Interior.
63. Electric Test Car.

MELLON INSTITUTE OF INDUSTRIAL RESEARCH:—

64. General View
65. Laboratory for two Research Fellows.
66. Laboratory for one Research Fellow.
67. Example of Unit Research Plant.

BUREAU OF STANDARDS:—

68. General View.
69. Engineering Building.
70. Electrical Building.

Plate.
BUREAU OF STANDARDS—*cont.*

71. Physical Testing Machine.
72. Tests on Masonry Pillar.
73. Tests on Lattice Girder.
74. Experimental Cement Kiln.

CARNEGIE INSTITUTION:—

75. Geophysical Laboratory.
76. Laboratory for Terrestrial Magnetism.

FOREST PRODUCTS LABORATORY:—

77. General View.
78. Wood Preservation Plant.
79. Paper Making Plant.
80. Chemical By-products Plant.

INSTITUTE OF INDUSTRIAL RESEARCH, WASHINGTON.

81. General View.

ELECTRICAL TESTING LABORATORIES:—

82. General View.
83. Lamp Testing Laboratory.
84. Private Research Laboratory.

FITZGERALD LABORATORIES:—

85. Corner of Furnace Laboratory.

INDUSTRIAL RESEARCH IN THE UNITED STATES.

INTRODUCTION.

The purpose of this memorandum is twofold. It is intended primarily to furnish a record of some observations relating to industrial research as conducted in the United States. To this end descriptions are given of the laboratories in various works, and in educational, State, and private institutions, with a statement of the endowment funds available, and a discussion of legislative and other influences tending towards the nationalisation of research, and of the methods of selecting and training scientific investigators, and co-ordinating their activities and results. The experience so related suggests naturally the consideration of our own country's position in similar matters, and to the account of what is being done in the United States a discussion in very general terms is subjoined, outlining some fundamental considerations which indicate the increasing necessity for research in this country, and offering some suggestions regarding the development of such work, and the relation which any comprehensive national scheme should bear to British industries and to research institutions in the Overseas Dominions.

The term "Industrial Research" is usually held to imply those investigations which have a direct bearing on the development of industry. It must not, however, be overlooked that a discovery made in pure science to-day may find application in industry to-morrow, and that such industrial application, though its precise form cannot always be foreseen at the time, has come to be an expected incident in the after-life of the discovery.

In this memorandum the wide view is taken that in considering the needs of industry pure science research is as essential as that specifically devoted to the attainment of some industrial objective. Though only brief reference is made to contemporary research in sciences where the connection with industry is not obvious, the greatest importance is attached to such investigations. They may provide raw material for industrial research, and, owing to the interdependence of modern investigations, progress in one science may have a marked bearing on developments in others.

The main difference between those researches that are undertaken for the purpose of furnishing material for industrial development and those undertaken by scientific men for the purpose of widening the boundaries of human knowledge, is that industrial research is becoming definitely organised to cover certain fields of science, while research in pure science is more spontaneous and depends more on the initiative and will of individual workers.

No attempt has been made to record extensively the extremely interesting work of the various laboratories visited. The aim has been to note those features and that trend of development in the United States which appear to bear on our own national problem, due regard being paid to the difference in character of the industrial conditions in this country compared with those in the United States, and to the fact that extensive though little known research work is being carried out in Great Britain, in addition to valuable research in pure science, for which this country holds a pre-eminent place.

I.—CLASSIFICATION OF INDUSTRIAL RESEARCH LABORATORIES.

Industrial research in the United States may be classified according to whether it is undertaken by—
Manufacturing corporations,
Associations of manufacturers,
Universities and colleges, including the Mellon Institute of Industrial Research,
National institutions,
Commercial laboratories,
Scientific societies.

II.—MANUFACTURING CORPORATIONS.

By far the most extensive research of a purely industrial character is that carried out by manufacturing corporations. Very marked developments in this respect have taken place during the past ten years. Capitalists who have derived benefit from the application of science in industry have not been content to await chance discoveries, but have established their own laboratories and research staffs. Further incentives in this direction have been provided by the industrial progress achieved in Europe by similar means, and by the influx of many scientifically trained men from Germany. Further, a tendency towards national economy and a fear of the depletion of natural resources have directed attention to the importance of scientific conservation of these assets. In some cases large industrial corporations have found it expedient for political reasons to keep before the public the fact that investigations on a large scale ultimately bring considerable benefit to the community generally ; that every scientific discovery applied in industry reacts to the public gain ; and that consequently industrial trusts are justified, since it is only where there are large aggregations of capital that the most extensive and productive research facilities can be maintained.

At present there are a large number of manufacturing corporations whose annual expenditure on research ranges from 10,000*l*. to 100,000*l*., and the tendency for each large industrial firm is towards the establishment of its own research laboratory.

The research work thus commenced by manufacturing corporations appears to develop through certain more or less well-defined stages, according to the character of the industry. These stages may be defined as follows :—

a) Research applied to the elimination of manufacturing troubles.

In manufacturing organisations some difficulties regarding materials and methods inevitably arise, tending to prevent smooth working. To overcome these difficulties, some investigation is necessary, which, if done thoroughly, involves analysis of the cause of the trouble and hence leads to its elimination. Some manufacturers in such cases are content to apply rule-of-thumb methods, which, while effecting a temporary alleviation, do not preclude a fresh outbreak of similar trouble in the same or some other form. Progressive firms provide organised means for investigating and eliminating such manufacturing troubles, and the extent to which it is necessary to apply science to this end depends on the nature of the product and the complexity of the manufacturing processes. In the largest manufacturing firms of every industry there is usually ample scope for a scientific staff and laboratory facilities to deal with such troubles.

(b) Research having some new and specific commercial object.

This kind of research involves an intelligent appreciation of the trend of development of manufacture and the possible applications of a product, and a close study of the scientific features and new discoveries that will pave the way for its successful manufacture. Frequently the appreciation of the need in industry for some new tool, method, or material, stimulates a deliberate search for means to satisfy that demand. Or again, the development of manufacturing methods for producing commodities heretofore brought to a high state of perfection in some other locality or country may involve the development of tools and processes of which no previous experience has been obtained.

Many important firms have been sufficiently far-sighted to provide extensively for research of this character, and such facilities have been turned to very profitable account in connection with new industries developed since the outbreak of the European War. In many cases these laboratories not only supply the works with new inventions and discoveries, but are used to carry on the manufacture of products with which the works themselves are not well suited to deal. In fact, it is said that in some industries the research laboratory is not considered successful unless it can pay its own way out of the profits arising from the sale of commodities thus produced.

(c) Researches in pure science with no specific commercial application in view.

Among the most progressive firms there is a growing appreciation of the fact that almost every discovery in science ultimately may have influence on industry. Such firms devote increasing attention to research of this character, and in some cases special laboratories have been installed quite distinct from the ordinary research laboratory for this purpose. This may be viewed as a very far-seeing business policy, directed to outstripping competition by the continuous provision of discoveries, which may sooner or later be turned to industrial account. It is recognised that in such cases there is a probability of a great deal of the new scientific knowledge thus obtained being only of limited use to the particular industry concerned. On the other hand, one successful discovery may result in such important industrial gains as to outweigh by far the cost of all the abortive research.

(d) **Research applied to public service.**

Many industries and public utility companies find that the market for their products can be profitably increased by a careful investigation of their customers' needs. Especially does this appear to be the case with electrical power supply companies, some of which maintain research laboratories for the investigation of new uses for electrical energy.

(e) **Research for the purpose of establishing standard methods of testing and standard specifications connected with the purchase of raw materials.**

Many large firms carry out a considerable amount of investigation mainly with this object in view, and efforts of this kind are to a considerable extent rendered of common value through the channels afforded by the American Society for Testing Materials, of which the leading corporations are members.

III.—EXAMPLES OF INDUSTRIAL RESEARCH LABORATORIES OF MANUFACTURING CORPORATIONS.

The following are a few typical examples of research laboratories connected with manufacturing corporations in such industries as steel, electrical, mechanical and general engineering, railway, automobile, chemical, rubber, glass, photographic and electrical power supply.

The description of each laboratory, both in this section and later, is given without reference to the laboratories of other bodies. This involves in some cases the repetition of features that are common to more than one institution. But it gives a clearer picture of the resources of the several establishments; and the recurrence of the features that they have in common is in itself of some significance, and may perhaps be emphasised with advantage.

It will be noted that whereas some firms maintain separate laboratories for routine control work and research, others carry out both kinds of investigations in the same laboratories, and in some cases utilise the works' equipment for research on a scale that is beyond the capacity of the usual experimental facilities.

American Rolling Mill Company, Middletown, O.

This company controls several works, and is one of the largest producers of sheet iron and steel in the United States. An important product of the company is high quality magnetic sheet steel, and another is a rustless form of sheet iron.

The company's laboratories comprise those for chemical and fuel testing in the various works, in which routine work and the elimination of manufacturing troubles are dealt with. There is also a separate laboratory devoted solely to research work, an illustration of which is shown in Plate 1. In connection with the latter laboratory there are outdoor proving grounds for testing the weather-resisting properties of certain sheet products.

PLATE 1.—Research Building, American Rolling Mill Company.

PLATE 2.—Magnetic Laboratory, American Rolling Mill Company.

PLATE 3.—Photomicrographic Laboratory, American Rolling Mill Company.

PLATE 4.—Physical and Electrical Laboratory, Ansonia, American Brass Company.

While some research work was commenced as early as 1901, the present laboratory was not completed until 1910. It comprises a three-story building 40 by 60 feet, the cost of which, together with equipment, was approximately 9,000*l*. The annual maintenance cost is about 10,000*l*. The laboratory includes divisions for chemical, electro-magnetic, metallurgical, photomicrographic, and physical investigations. A portion of the magnetic laboratory is shown in Plate 2, and Plate 3 shows the division dealing with photomicrographic work.

The staff numbers about 15, the majority of whom are University graduates. In addition to the permanent staff the services of a number of eminent metallurgists in England, Germany, and the United States are from time to time employed. As occasion demands, special research work is carried out for the company by some of the universities and commercial research laboratories possessing special facilities. A 5-ton open-hearth furnace is available in the works in order that the investigations of the research laboratory may be continued on a manufacturing scale whenever this is found desirable.

Research is directed mainly to the investigation of manufacturing troubles and to the discovery of new sheet ferrous products for which a demand, actual or potential, exists. Comparatively little work is done in pure science. On the other hand, a speciality is made of investigations for the service of customers. For instance, extended researches were made with a view to developing a suitable sheet material for motor car work, which could be enamelled cheaply and possess a surface yielding a very high degree of finish.

The research department has been made the centre of an organisation for collecting and distributing to the manufacturing departments all published information of a scientific character bearing on the company's work.

The American Brass Company, Waterbury, Conn.

Several works directed to the production of brass and other alloys, many of which are used in the electrical industry, are controlled by this company. There are three principal laboratories connected with the company's works at Ansonia, Waterbury, and Kenosha respectively. The company possesses no laboratory specially devoted to research, although a considerable amount of scientific investigation is carried on in the regular laboratories, together with routine testing.

Plate 4 shows a general view of the physical and electrical laboratory of Ansonia, where a staff of 8 technical men is employed. Plate 5 shows a portion of the chemical laboratory at Waterbury, which is specially devoted to electrolytic investigations. In this laboratory there are altogether 27 people employed. In the smaller laboratory at Kenosha there is a staff of 5.

Detroit Edison Company, Detroit, Mich.

This company supplies electrical energy to the city of Detroit and the surrounding district. Its size may be judged from the fact that at present it has a peak load of about 100,000 K.V.A. The company has found it advantageous to maintain a research department for the scientific investigation of problems arising in connection with the efficient running of the organisation, and also for the service of customers who seek to employ electrical energy for special purposes.

The researches thus far carried out include those dealing with steel tube condensers; experimental development of a heater-condenser of the spray type; relative values of steam pipe covering; the growth of crystals in steel boiler tubes working on high rating; new methods of japanning, and, in particular, the electro-chemistry of japan baking; new forms of resistance heaters; new types of electric furnaces; electric methods of heating, treating, and annealing metals, &c. One interesting investigation of considerable utility has been that dealing with the problem of maintaining economically a suitable temperature in private garages in the winter time when the atmospheric temperature is about zero. This investigation has involved experiments with the heat-retaining properties of walls, floors, and roofs, and the adaptation of electric thermostats to the maintenance of a uniform temperature.

The results of some of the researches of the company have been published.

Consequent upon research many new uses have been found for electrical energy, and the service of the company has thus been considerably extended.

The technical members of the company's research staff include a chief and three assistants. There is also a field staff composed of engineers, detailed by one or other of the operating or construction departments, to carry out investigations required under the direction of the research department. Several outside engineers are either permanently or temporarily retained, such as those associated with colleges or universities. Some research has also been done in co-operation with the United States Bureau of Mines.

The company maintains certain fellowships, each for a period of one year, at the University of Michigan. The holders are required to carry out research work of an approved character.

Dodge Bros., Detroit, Mich.

The laboratories of this company are typical of a large and progressive manufacturing concern. About 25 men are employed in the chemical, physical, metallographical, and pyrometric laboratories, the equipment of which cost about 5,000*l*. While these facilities are primarily directed towards testing and controlling the materials and supplies for the plant and its products, a good deal of research work is being done on problems affecting the industry.

Du Pont de Nemours and Company, Wilmington, Delaware.

This company is engaged extensively in the manufacture of explosives and other chemicals. Its chemical department comprises three main divisions, namely, a field division for investigations outside the laboratory in connection with manufacturing operations; an experimental station for research work in connection with manufacturing problems and in the development of new processes; and a laboratory which is confined to research connected with high explosives.

Upwards of 250 chemists are employed, and very considerable profits are said to be made from the products of the laboratories themselves.

PLATE 5.—Electrolytic Laboratory, Waterbury, American Brass Company.

PLATE 6.—Research Building, Eastman Kodak Company.

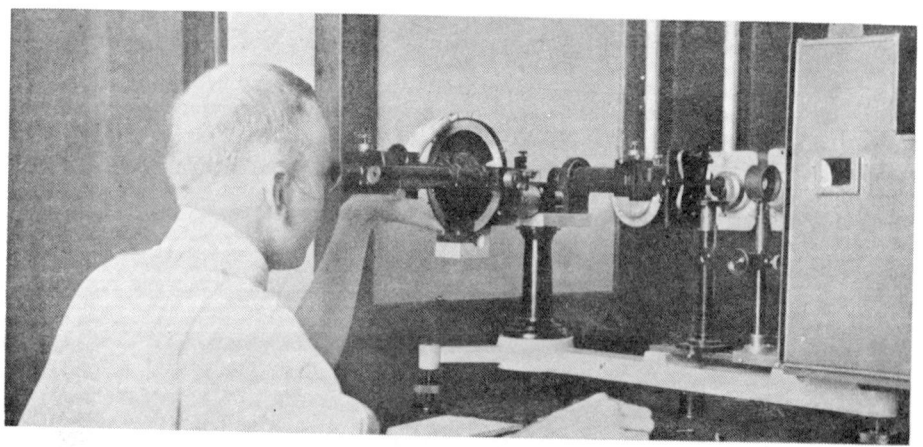

PLATE 7.—Plant for Plate Manufacture, Eastman Kodak Company.

PLATE 8.—Spectrophotometer, Eastman Kodak Company.

Eastman Kodak Company, Rochester, N.Y.

This company is one of the largest producers of photographic apparatus, chemicals, papers, films, etc. A very extensive research building, shown in Plate 6, was erected about three years ago partly for the purpose of carrying out such scientific investigations as were necessary to control manufacturing processes, but more especially for original research of a purely scientific character, such as would enable the company to maintain its position in the front rank of the photographic industry.

The first cost of the laboratory was about 30,000*l*.; the present annual maintenance cost is about the same amount, this being approximately 0 7 per cent. of the company's annual profits.

The staff numbers approximately 40, of whom about 15 are specialists of high scientific standing.

The laboratory comprises a number of divisions dealing with physics; inorganic, organic, and colloidal chemistry; optics; colour photography; film problems; general photography, including cinematographic work; chemical products and emulsions and coating preparations.

An important feature of the laboratory is its manufacturing section, in which the processes developed experimentally are carried out on a practical scale prior to being turned over to the works manufacturing departments. This section includes emulsion processes and plate, film, and paper-coating departments, the plate department alone, illustrated in Plate 7, having a capacity of upwards of 3,000 plates per day. Apart from full-scale experiments of this kind, chemical products and photographic accessories required in small quantities for special purposes—as, for instance, spectroscopic, astronomical, colour photography, etc.—are dealt with in the laboratory. In this way the works are relieved from non-standard products which would involve delay and disorganisation.

The scientific work is directed by means of daily conferences, each day of the week being assigned to some general subject, the main divisions being physics, photography, and chemistry. The work of the physics laboratory is divided into several parts, dealing respectively with spectroscopy, photometry and sensitometry, the latter being concerned with the measurement of the sensitiveness of photographic products. Plate 8 shows an instrument for determining the opacity of coloured films and light-filters, and Plate 9 indicates a new form of electrical control for automatic sensitometers.

Intermediate between the work of the physics and photographic departments, is that of the large projection room containing long optical instruments. Plate 10 shows photomicrographic apparatus, cinematographic projection machine and projection spectroscope. In this room the focal lengths and aberrations of lenses are measured, with an accuracy previously unobtainable, on a lens-testing bench designed and constructed in the laboratory.

The top floor of the laboratory building is devoted to photographic work, studios for portraiture and colour photography, and also for copying, photo-engraving and commercial photography. Plate 11 shows a remarkably complex electrical apparatus for the measurement of reduction potential in an investigation on the physico-chemical properties of developers. Plate 12 indicates a laboratory for the preparation of photographic solutions.

A very important section of the work is concerned with electro-chemistry, electro-analysis, and colloidal chemistry. Plate 13 gives a general view of this department. For researches in colloidal chemistry a number of special instruments, thermostats, refrigerators, ultra-microscope, and other special optical devices are installed. Plate 14 shows a variety of viscosimeters used in this work.

The remaining chemical laboratories are set apart from the main building so that the fumes evolved may not interfere with the delicate photographic emulsions dealt with in the laboratory building itself. Plate 15 shows an organic laboratory furnished with plant for performing processes such as nitrations, reductions, etc.

A monthly bulletin is published, giving a list of patents and an abstract of the most important papers appearing in the technical journals associated with the photographic industry. A great many of the results of the researches carried out are published in the scientific press, and the laboratory on the whole is considered to be one of the finest of its kind. An extensive library is maintained for the use of the research staff.

General Electric Company, Schenectady, N.Y.

This company comprises a number of separate works, and manufactures all kinds of electrical machinery and apparatus. It is one of the largest organisations of its kind in the world. A number of laboratories are maintained, principally in connection with the production problems of the different works. These comprise experimental facilities for the development of illuminating engineering; the investigation of high tension phenomena; physical and chemical investigations of materials and instrument developments.

For research work a laboratory was commenced on a small scale about 14 years ago at an annual maintenance cost of about 1,000*l*. The annual cost of research work now is from 80,000*l*. to 100,000*l*., and a staff of upwards of 150 is employed. The present research laboratory occupies the first five floors of the seven-story building shown in Plate 16.

This laboratory, which is world-famed, comprises a large number of divisions dealing with the experimental development of such materials as porcelain; insulating compounds; high quality magnetic steels; rare metals such as tungsten, molybdenum, boron, and their alloys; carbons for electrical illumination; wireless apparatus; X-ray tubes. There are also complete laboratories for chemical analysis and physical testing.

Equipment is provided on a commercial manufacturing scale for lamps, X-ray tubes, the preparation of tungsten and other rare metals, various electric furnace products, and for specialities with which the manufacturing departments of the works are not readily adapted to deal.

Typical laboratories for the investigation of insulating materials and for the investigation of magnetic steels are shown in Plate 17 and Plate 18 respectively. A separate building shown in Plate 19 includes in its equipment porcelain kilns,

PLATE 9.—Automatic Sensitometer Control, Eastman Kodak Company.

PLATE 10.—Large Projection Room, Eastman Kodak Company.

PLATE 11.—Research Work in Developers, Eastman Kodak Company.

PLATE 12.—Photographic Laboratory, Eastman Kodak Company.

calorising furnaces and a sixty-ton hydraulic press. Very extensive laboratory equipment is provided in each of the branches of research dealt with. For instance, the laboratories for insulation investigations are provided with various grinders, mixers, impregnating plant, and high-voltage testing apparatus. In the magnetic laboratories there are various electric furnaces for heat treatment, photomicrographic apparatus, etc. The division dealing with the manufacture of Coolidge X-ray tubes is equipped with molecular pumps, static machine, fluoroscopic and stereoscopic apparatus. A part of the equipment of this laboratory is shown in Plate 20.

The illuminating laboratories comprise colour booth; photometric equipment; means for the production and purification of argon; furnaces for the reduction of tungsten oxide, etc. A portion of this latter laboratory is shown in Plate 21.

There is a well-equipped machine shop for the needs of the laboratory, and a very extensive library is also provided. The floor space of the laboratory totals about 66,000 sq. ft.

In addition to the equipment of the individual laboratories, the building as a whole is piped throughout with gas, air, high and low pressure hydrogen, oxygen, vacuum, steam, and distilled water.

A notable feature of the laboratory is its equipment for the manufacture on a commercial scale of new products developed which are of a character not readily suited to the facilities of the works, such manufacture being carried on until it reaches a magnitude that justifies the setting up of factories specially for the purpose.

It is important to note that the experience of the workers in this laboratory has been that investigations in pure science lead almost inevitably, in course of time, to some commercial application, and increasing attention is therefore being paid to this phase of research work.

It is generally acknowledged that the research laboratory has been an unquestionable financial success, not only because it has solved regularly the industrial problems of the large organisation with which it is connected, but also because it has produced discoveries which the company can turn to advantage. It sells annually large quantities of valuable products arising directly from the discoveries made in the laboratory and manufactured therein. Moreover, several new factories have been started to undertake work that has grown beyond the scope of the manufacturing departments of the laboratory, and enormously valuable work has been carried out in connection with the illuminating industry, which has led to a wide and very profitable manufacture for this company. Further, the research department is able to pronounce authoritatively, for the benefit of capitalists, on the probabilities of success of new projects involving considerations of a scientific character.

The policy in connection with the staff of the laboratory has been to employ highly trained mathematical physicists, and particularly men of breadth of view, who are sufficiently visionary and appreciative of the enormous industrial possibilities of scientific discoveries.

The results of much of the research work, particularly that with the character of pure science, are widely published in the scientific press, and in the *General Electric Review*.

The laboratory serves as a scientific focus of a number of different industries, and on a small scale represents the lines on which a national plan of industrial research might be based.

Pittsfield Works.—This factory of the General Electric Company deals mainly with the manufacture of transformers, small motors, and electrical heating apparatus. The most striking feature of its equipment of a research character is a high-tension testing plant, capable of dealing with voltages up to 750,000. This equipment is housed in a special building, and forms one of the most complete high-tension laboratories of this kind in existence. A great deal of extremely valuable research work has been carried out in this laboratory.

General Motors Company, Detroit, Mich.

This company is engaged in automobile manufacture. Its laboratories comprise sections devoted to chemical, metallurgical, physical, mechanical, and electrical testing, and a staff of about 20 is employed. In each division much routine work is carried on, but in addition there is a good deal of research directed to objects of value to the automobile industry. The research side of the laboratory work has been developed very considerably of late, and it is probable that in the near future the company's activities in this respect will rank with those of other prominent industrial firms.

The present laboratory floor space is about 10,000 sq. ft.

The chemical laboratory is equipped for analysis and investigation of iron, steel, brass, bronze, organic materials and fuel. The metallurgical laboratory contains apparatus for the heat treatment of metals, photomicrographic work, pyrometry, etc. The electrical laboratory is provided with tensile testing machines up to 200,000 lbs. capacity, alternating stress testing machines of various types, a torsion machine, cold bend, shot test and drop test apparatus.

The mechanical laboratory is equipped with special dynamometer stands for automobile work, and there is also a machine shop for work connected with the laboratory.

The B.F. Goodrich Company, Akron, O.

Rubber tyres are manufactured by this company, and its laboratories are devoted solely to rubber investigations. Some of these investigations are of a purely commercial character, but a great deal of valuable research work is also undertaken.

This may be classified in three divisions, namely—

(1) Research dealing with the examination and synthetic preparation of raw materials. There are three laboratories connected with this division:—

(a) A chemical laboratory for the testing of all raw materials.

(b) A research laboratory for chemical analysis, equipped, in addition to the usual chemical apparatus, with experimental size mills, calenders, presses, etc., in order to prepare on a practical scale the materials to be specially investigated.

(c) A special research laboratory in which specially treated rubbers and pigments are prepared and tested.

PLATE 13.—Physico-Chemical Laboratory, Eastman Kodak Company.

PLATE 14.—Laboratory for Colloidal Chemistry, Eastman Kodak Company.

PLATE 15.—Organic Laboratory, Eastman Kodak Company.

PLATE 16.—Research Building, General Electric Company.

(2) A division which deals with the research connected with the application of raw materials to specific lines of manufacture and consists of two sections :—

    (*a*) A physical testing laboratory containing yarn and fabric testers, elongation and tensile testing machines, and mill room equipped with a model factory containing presses, washers, dryers, kneading machine, tool machine, spreader, hose rubber, and experimental mills and calenders, in which on a small scale articles may be produced just as is done in the factory, so that manufacturing methods may be developed.

    (*b*) A section comprising a force of technically trained engineers, who handle problems arising out of the use of rubber compounds in the factory, and who deal with the construction of new compounds to meet the particular requirements of the trade.

(3) A division which consists of a physical research laboratory in charge of a highly trained physicist, and is equipped with all apparatus necessary for rubber investigations.

The complete staff of the laboratories numbers about 150, and it ranks among the best of its kind in connection with the rubber industry.

International Acheson Graphite Company, Niagara Falls, N.Y.

This company manufactures graphite for lubricants, electrodes, crucibles, etc. Its research department is staffed by six men of scientific training. Much of the investigation is done on the actual works plant, especially that requiring the use of electric furnaces, and in this way it is carried out on a semi-commercial scale.

Research connected with lubricants is dealt with in a laboratory specially devoted to that purpose.

The products of the company are entirely special, and a great deal of important research has been done in connection with their development.

A chemical laboratory is provided for dealing with general analytical work.

National Carbon Company, Cleveland, O.

A number of different works are controlled by this company, which manufactures carbon specialities, particularly those connected with electrical work, such as arc lamp carbons, brushes, battery carbons and rheostats. The largest works, and the one which contains the most extensive laboratories, is situated at Cleveland, Ohio. There the laboratory staff engaged on scientific work numbers 62 men, who have received the major portion of their training in the universities.

The laboratories are divided into three main groups, concerned respectively with—

    Analysis and control,
    Fundamental research, and
    Factory development.

The analytical laboratory deals with all routine analytical and control work of a chemical nature. There are two main divisions, applying respectively to illuminating work and problems connected mainly with tests on illuminating carbons. The main function of the analytical and control laboratories is to ensure uniformity of quality of the products of the company.

The function of the research laboratory is to study the fundamental principles involved in the manufacture and utilisation of the company's products, and to indicate how these principles may be employed in improving existing processes and products. Every effort is made not only to devise new products but also to extend the field of application of the present ones.

The development division of the laboratory forms the connecting link between the research laboratory and the factory, in that it is devoted to undertaking on a small commercial scale processes conceived in the research laboratory, and if success is assured, transferring them to the works. This division also investigates manufacturing operations and carries out experimental work in the factory itself. Some of this work has resulted in development of much labour-saving machinery.

Among the investigations with which the laboratories as a whole have dealt are those relating to carbon regulating rheostats; brushes for electrical machines; arc carbons for projecting work in connection with cinematographs; electrodes for the flame arc lamp; special electrodes for use in connection with lamps for photomicrographic, spectrographic, and photo-chemical effects; the comparative fading action of sunlight and white flame arcs on various dyes used by clothing and textile manufacturers; electrodes used in connection with colour matching.

While much of this research work is of a confidential nature, from time to time various results are published.

The laboratories are equipped with a very complete library, and all means are taken to acquire up-to-date information from the home and foreign scientific journals connected with the subjects under investigation.

National Cash Register Company, Dayton, O.

This company virtually possesses the monopoly of the manufacture of cash-registering apparatus. Its research laboratory comprises very complete chemical, physical, and microscopic testing outfits, and a staff of about 15 is employed. Two-thirds of the men are scientifically trained.

The aim of the laboratory which determines the character of its work is the careful scientific elimination of troubles arising in the course of manufacture and in the improvement of the materials employed. A great deal of attention is paid, for instance, to the careful study of the wearing properties of various metals used in the cash register and their behaviour under repeatedly applied stresses. Plate 22 shows a machine undergoing such a test. Very little work is done in pure science.

Under the control of the research department there is a small laboratory for the production of special inks used by the firm.

The work of the laboratory has led to considerable improvements in the quality and cheapness of the raw materials employed, but the most striking feature is the scientific manner in which manufacturing difficulties are investigated.

PLATE 17.—Laboratory for Insulation Research, General Electric Company.

PLATE 18.—Laboratory for Magnetic Research, General Electric Company.

PLATE 19.—Furnace Room, General Electric Company.

PLATE 20.—Laboratory for Coolidge X-Ray Tubes, General Electric Company.

National Electric Lamp Association, Cleveland, O.

This association, which is controlled by the General Electric Company, comprises some twenty or more electric lamp factories in different parts of the States. A common research laboratory has been established in connection with these companies. The laboratory buildings, together with those used for sales and administrative purposes, comprise seven large blocks of four or five floors each, situated in a park of 79 acres.

The employees number in all about six hundred, and about one-third of the total capacity in buildings and staff appears to be devoted to laboratory work. Plate 23 shows a portion of some of the buildings and the character of the surroundings.

The work of the laboratory comprises the testing of materials for electric lamp manufacture, the design of new models, the investigation of new illuminating problems, including those relating to colour matching, photographic work, electric signs, photometry, moving pictures and the illumination of buildings. A great point is made of dealing with customers' problems by a staff of experts, who are sent out to study local conditions and prepare designs and specifications for illuminating work. The greatest attention is given to improving the efficiency of domestic lamps, having in mind the enormous aggregate saving that even a small improvement in power consumption involves. Plate 24 shows the engineering building, in which much of this laboratory work is carried on.

A most striking feature of the laboratory is its full-scale manufacturing plant for producing electric lamps in bulk, by which means manufacturing methods are perfected and the necessary automatic tools produced. This model factory is contained in a building 450 by 50 ft., having four floors. In this part of the laboratory manual operations are studied scientifically, and complete manufacturing information drawn up and made available for all the different companies of the association, who can thus devote their entire attention to manufacture without being hampered by experimental work. In this manner consistency of quality can be maintained throughout the entire organisation, each branch of which has the assistance of the leading experts in illuminating work.

Co-operation exists between all the different companies of the association in regard to receiving suggestions and working out new ideas that may be sent up from any one of them to this central laboratory. The researches in this laboratory are made available to other companies interested that are controlled by the General Electric Company, in particular the Edison Electric Lamp Works at Harrison, N.J.

Connected with the association in a separate building is the Nela Research Laboratory, shown in Plate 25. The laboratory was organised at the end of 1908 for the investigation of those problems in the sciences of physics, physiology, and psychology which might have bearing on the science of light. The object of the laboratory has been primarily to acquire new knowledge rather than to develop commercial processes or commodities. The building is approximately 128 by 38 ft. in floor space, and has two stories. There is a small section which is devoted to applied science and organised for the investigation of certain physical problems which might have practical application, this being the only portion of the laboratory whose work is admittedly commercial in its aim.

In addition to the director of the laboratory the present staff in the pure science section comprises five physicists, one psychologist, and one physiologist, and in the section of applied science two physicists. These are all scientific men of high standing. There are in addition a number of assistants, with a mechanical and office staff.

The researches are initiated mainly by the director of the laboratory, and fall into three broad groups:—

(a) Those dealing with the production of luminous energy.
(b) Those dealing with the utilisation of luminous energy.
(c) Those investigating the effects of luminous and attendant radiation.

The research men meet frequently for discussions of the problems undertaken, and the results of the various investigations appear in the scientific press. Abstracts of all papers emanating from the laboratory are published in a bulletin issued by the laboratory from time to time. The total number of scientific papers published during the past eight years amounts approximately to 125. These papers are of a very high order of excellence, and rank among the most authoritative work in connection with the science of illumination.

In addition to the regular staff of the laboratory there have been each year a number of outside research workers, who spend some time in carrying out their investigations in the laboratory. For instance, a number of university professors are invited each summer to work there for a period of several months, while others with problems of interest are accorded the facilities of the laboratory for pursuing their researches.

During the past year and a half three men have been in residence at the laboratory as holders of the C. F. Brush Fellowships in Physics. At the present time there are seven research men, outside of the regular staff, carrying on investigations in the laboratory. Plate 26 shows a general view of one section of the physical laboratory.

The institution of this laboratory in connection with an industrial concern is indicative of a very broad-minded policy, and one that is likely to have far-reaching effects, not only in the ultimate benefit to the public, but also in laying the foundations of the future prosperity and supremacy of the association, which is in the best possible position to profit by the scientific discoveries made.

New Jersey Zinc Company, New York, N.Y.

There is a research laboratory at one of the branches of this company, having a technical staff of 11 men. This laboratory comprises divisions for chemical analysis and photomicrographic work. It undertakes also operations intermediate between those of the laboratory and the factory.

The work of the laboratory consists mainly in the study of different manufacturing processes and the application of the products of the company in connection with paint, rubber goods, galvanising and the manufacture of alloys. The plant comprises also equipment for manufacturing and testing various products on a small working scale under the direction of the research department.

PLATE 21.—Tungsten Reduction Furnaces, General Electric Company.

PLATE 22.—Register Testing Machine, National Cash Register Company.

PLATE 23.—General View of Laboratories and Park, National Electric Lamp Association.

PLATE 24.—Engineering Building, National Electric Lamp Association.

Pennsylvania Railroad Company, Altoona, Pa.

Very extensive research laboratories are maintained by this company at Altoona, and a staff numbering in all 361 is employed. Of these, 282 men are employed in the physical laboratory, half of whom are engaged on the inspection of materials and construction work, and the rest on physical testing and research work. About one-fourth of the latter group are technical graduates. The remaining 79 men are attached to the chemical laboratory, and about two-thirds of these have received technical training.

The technical staff is drawn from all the leading universities and technical colleges in the States, and also includes some men from technological institutions in Europe.

A general view of the main laboratory building is shown in Plate 27. The cost of buildings and equipment amounted approximately to 60,000*l*. There is in addition a locomotive testing plant, shown in Plate 28, the approximate cost of which was 40,000*l*. The annual maintenance cost of the laboratories is approximately 100,000*l*., this sum including labour and material, but not the cost of transportation of field inspectors over the whole of the railway system.

Close co-operation exists between the laboratory and the Bureau of Standards at Washington, also with the American Society for Testing Materials, the Master Car Builders' Association, the American Rail Masters Mechanics Association, and the American Society of Mechanical Engineers. The laboratory has carried out the bulk of the research work required by certain of these associations.

The function of the laboratory is to minimise or eliminate railway accidents traceable to defective or unsuitable material, and much of the investigation is directed to the preparation of specifications framed in order to safeguard the quality of the materials supplied.

A department for physical testing was first established by this company in 1874. The present laboratory was completed in 1914. It has a floor area of 41,000 sq. ft., and comprises four floors and a basement. The first floor is devoted to physical tests, and contains a laboratory equipped with five universal tension and compression testing machines, the largest of which has a capacity of 1,000,000 lbs. A general view of this laboratory is shown in Plate 30. The second floor is used largely for the office accommodation of the laboratory staff. The third floor is divided into laboratories for bacteriological, water, gas, and rubber analysis, and for photometry and the calibration of electrical instruments. The fourth floor is used for general chemical laboratories. The various laboratories are subdivided as follows :—

The physical laboratory deals with tests of all kinds of materials such as rubber, air-brake hose and springs. An illustration of one of the machines for testing springs is shown in Plate 29. This laboratory also contains special ovens for the heat treatment of steels, castings of various kinds, tie-plates etc. A general view of this division is shown in Plate 31. There is a separate laboratory for photomicrographic work.

The electrical laboratory is subdivided into sections for the standardisation of instruments, the carrying out of all kinds of general electrical investigations associated with railway work and lamp testing. Plate 32 shows one of the large photometric laboratories, and Plate 33 shows a laboratory for lamp testing.

A bacteriological laboratory is provided, and also laboratories for the testing of water and the investigation of disinfectants. A laboratory for the investigation of heat-insulating materials is shown in Plate 34.

The general chemical laboratory shown in Plate 35 comprises divisions for metallurgical work and miscellaneous investigations in connection with oils, lacquers, coating compounds, fire-extinguishing preparations and food products. There is also a small manufacturing laboratory which is virtually a model factory, in which new products are manufactured until outside suppliers can be found to undertake their preparation.

For field investigations a laboratory car is provided, a view of which is shown in Plate 36. This is equipped with full metallurgical and analytical testing appliances, and can be moved to wherever steel rails are in process of manufacture.

A fully equipped dynamometer car, an illustration of which is shown in Plate 37, is also available for field service.

There is at present being installed in a separate building a large brake shoe testing machine, having two dynamometers of 4,000 lbs. capacity. An illustration of this machine is shown in Plate 38.

The magnitude of the work of this laboratory is indicated by the fact that in 1913 the total cost of materials inspected and tested amounted to over 16,000,000l. The cost of operating the laboratory departments for the same year was rather more than 100,000l., *i.e.*, the total cost of the entire laboratory work, including inspection and testing, is about 0 6 per cent. of the cost of materials.

A most important feature of the research work is the preparation of purchasing specifications based on the results of careful laboratory investigations.

Much of the work of the laboratory has been published, in the form of purchasing specifications, in the proceedings of some of the associations already referred to. In addition to these, however, nearly 30 printed bulletins have been issued publicly from the laboratory; these deal with such subjects as fuel economy tests, super-heater tests, tonnage rating, brake tests, etc.

Reo Motor Company, Lansing, Mich.

The engineering department of this company employs about 65 people, and is separate from the manufacturing plant. In the department model cars are developed, built, and tested before final drawings are placed in the factory, which is thus not hampered with experimental work. Plate 39 shows the motors in the test bed.

Studebaker Corporation, South Bend, Ind.

This corporation manufactures automobiles and maintains two laboratories, one at its works at Detroit and the other at South Bend, Ind.

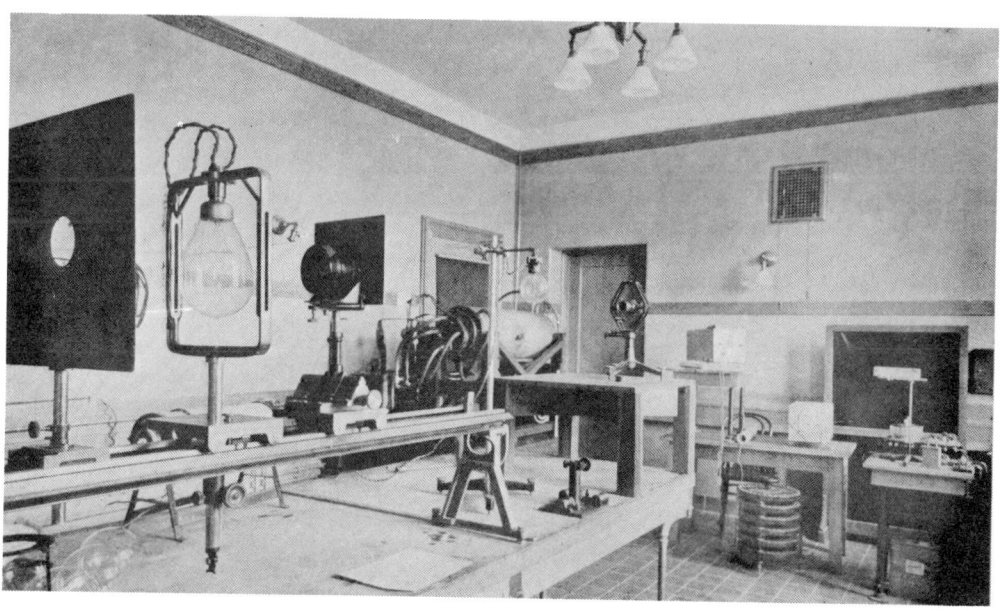

PLATE 25:—Physical Laboratory, National Electric Lamp Association.

PLATE 26.—Interior of Physical Laboratory, National Electric Lamp Association.

PLATE 27.—General View of Laboratory Building, Pennsylvania Railroad Company.

PLATE 28.—Locomotive Testing Laboratory, Pennsylvania Railroad Company.

At the Detroit laboratory there are about 15 men on the staff, five of whom are chemists, four metallurgists, and the remainder deal with work in the mechanical laboratory, and carry out special investigations in the shops. While much of the work of the laboratory is of a routine character, a considerable amount of research is being constantly undertaken, especially in connection with the heat treatment of the special steels required for automobile work. At the South Bend laboratory the work is largely of a routine character, and comprises investigations of paints, oils, varnishes, fabrics, etc., and the raw materials supplied to the foundry.

T. A. Edison Laboratories, East Orange, N.J.

The Edison laboratories are very extensive, and comprise some eight or more large blocks of four- or five-floor buildings. They consist in part of laboratories for the working out of new ideas and investigations under Mr. Edison's personal supervision, and in part of a factory for the commercial production of the inventions and commodities thus developed. In addition to these works, a number of separate factories have been started and are working solely on the production of materials or apparatus devised at East Orange. Important features of the works are a very fully equipped machine shop for the rapid production of new parts required in the working out of experimental apparatus, and a large commercial laboratory built 29 years ago, in which a vast amount of Mr. Edison's work has been done. Plate 40 shows an exterior view of this laboratory, and Plate 41 a portion of the interior

The greater part of the experimental work at East Orange is carried out in various parts of the factory buildings, according to the object or industry to which they are directed, and it is interesting to note that most of this work is conducted successfully on empirical lines, a marked contrast to modern research on a purely scientific basis.

Westinghouse Electric and Manufacturing Company, East Pittsburg, Pa.

This company manufactures all kinds of electrical machinery and apparatus. Its facilities for experimental investigations are very extensive, and in addition to laboratories employed for the control of various manufacturing products, there are several separate laboratories devoted solely to research work, much of it in pure science. These laboratories comprise divisions for chemical testing, a general view of which is shown in Plate 42. The laboratory for physical testing is shown in Plate 43, and the magnetic testing laboratory is shown in Plate 44. Another research laboratory devoted solely to high-tension investigations is shown in Plate 45.

A separate building, comprising three floors, is equipped entirely for fine electrical measurements. Experimental investigations in connection with moulded insulating materials are carried out in the laboratory shown in Plate 46, in which full scale manufacturing facilities are provided. These facilities include grinding, mixing, and moulding apparatus, also complete testing equipment for determining physical and electrical properties. In this laboratory complete processes can be evolved before work is attempted on a full manufacturing scale. For researches on a large engineering scale that are beyond the capacity of the research laboratory the works equipment is used. One such investigation is that shown in Plate 47, which illustrates research on extensive lines connected with the development of a vapour converter.

Similarly, Plate 48 shows the arrangements for some investigations carried out in the shops in connection with heavy flywheels.

A new research building is now in the course of construction, and is illustrated in its unfinished condition by Plate 49. This laboratory will accommodate a staff of about one hundred, and will be provided with facilities for magnetic, chemical, electro-chemical, and metallurgical research. Its equipment will cost about 30,000*l.*, and the annual total expenditure on research in this, together with the existing laboratories, will be from 70,000*l*. to 80,000*l*.

The research division of the company co-operates closely with the universities and other institutions that have facilities for special lines of investigation, or are concerned with the training of men for the company's research staff.

Many of the results of the research work carried out are published in the form of papers before the scientific societies or in the technical press.

Western Electric Company, New York, N.Y.

The technical development of the arts of telegraphy and telephony in the United States is directed mainly by two organisations, working in close co-operation, each with a distinct function to perform.

The American Telephone and Telegraph Company is responsible for the underlying· research work of a pure science character, while the manufacturing development is undertaken by the engineers of the Western Electric Company. The research work of the latter company is therefore of a utilitarian character, being aimed at the commercial development of specific apparatus. The former company investigates suggestions arising from the operating experience of the associated companies of the Bell Telephone System.

Approximately 40 per cent. of the thousand or more members of the laboratory staff of the Western Electric Company are technical graduates, and about 50 men are retained on research work proper, including investigations on acoustics, optics and radio-activity, as well as other physical, chemical, and metallurgical investigations. As might be expected in connection with a highly scientific industry, this work is of a very high order, and no expense is spared to secure the highest class of investigators and the best laboratory equipment.

Plate 50 shows part of the circuit laboratory used in studying the operation of telephone circuits. Plate 51 shows potentiometer and bridged apparatus in the transmission branch used in studying transmitters and receivers at speech frequencies, while Plate 52 shows artificial lines and other apparatus devoted to the study of loud-speaking telephones.

Other Companies.

Among other important companies doing considerable research work may be mentioned the American Locomotive Company, of Schenectady; also Bausch and Lomb Optical Company, Rochester, N.Y. This latter company manufactures optical

PLATE 29.—Spring Testing Laboratory, Pennsylvania Railroad Company.

PLATE 30.—Physical Laboratory, Pennsylvania Railroad Company.

PLATE 31.—Heat Treatment Laboratory, Pennsylvania Railroad Company.

instruments of all kinds, and carries out a great deal of original investigation, the results of which are issued from time to time in scientific and technical publications. The Goodyear Tire and Rubber Company, Akron, O., specialises in the manufacture of automobile and other tyres, and carries out a considerable amount of research work in this connection. It employs eight technical workers, and confines its investigations solely to problems presented in the rubber industries. One of the most prominent firms in that industry, the United States Rubber Company, carries on very extensive research work at New York. The Pittsburg Plate Glass Company, Creighton, Pa., carries out extensive research work in connection with this particular industry. Similar work is done by the United States Steel Corporation, the General Chemical Company, the United Gas Improvements Company, General Bakelite Company, etc.

Résumé of principal features.

The most striking features of the research work of the laboratories connected with industrial manufacturing corporations are :—

(a) The installation in many cases of full-scale manufacturing facilities, which on the one hand enables processes to be perfected and the works to be relieved of the hampering effects of experimental developments, and on the other hand gives the laboratory staff some elementary practical introduction to the complexities of actual manufacture as contrasted with the relative simplicity of laboratory preparation.

(b) The provision of manufacturing facilities in the laboratory in order to develop such products as result from new discoveries to the point at which the scale of manufacture calls for transfer to one of the works departments or to a new or separate organisation.

(c) The growing tendency to devote more and more of the resources of the laboratories to pure science investigations with a view to making discoveries. Such discoveries produce industrial developments which will facilitate progress in industries already established, or secure priority in some new industrial field.

(d) The freedom with which results of investigations in pure science are published by those at whose expense the work has been accomplished.

(e) The growing appreciation of men with scientific training not only in the research laboratory, where such training is essential, but also in regular manufacturing employment.

(f) The value of research laboratories as a means of inspiring confidence in the minds of customers, as an effective advertisement, and as evidence of up-to-date working which enhances the standing of the company with which they are connected.

(g) The employment of the laboratories by financiers for the purpose of ascertaining the merits of new industrial propositions of which the value has not been commercially established.

(h) The appreciation of the fact that well-conducted research laboratories on a large scale are sound financial propositions, as indicated by the increase in the number of such laboratories as part of the establishments of large firms.

(i) The fact that while the lavish expenditure of money in many of the research laboratories appears to be wasteful, and a great deal of work done which leads to no immediate financial return, the results of a single investigation may be of such far-reaching value in industry as to pay for all the abortive investigations.

IV.—ASSOCIATIONS OF MANUFACTURERS.

There are a number of associations of manufacturers in various industries which undertake research work for the common benefit of their members. Some of this work has been confined to the collection and distribution of home and foreign trade information. Among such associations are—

The Hardwood Lumber Association.
The National Association of Paint Manufacturers.
American Association of Woollen and Worsted Manufacturers.
National Canners' Association.
American Paper and Pulp Manufacturers' Association.
National Association of Refrigeration.
National Dairy Union.
Association of American Portland Cement Manufacturers.
Associated Metal Lath Manufacturers.
Gypsum Industries Association.
National Lime Manufacturers' Association.
Hollow Tile Manufacturers' Association.
National Brick Manufacturers' Association.

In some instances research work has been undertaken in laboratories connected with individual manufacturers, in universities, or at the Bureau of Standards. In others, the associations have provided their own common research laboratory, as, for instance, the National Canners' Association, a brief description of whose research work is as follows :—

National Canners' Association, Washington, D.C.

This association comprises manufacturers of materials and containers for the packing of foods, and includes such firms as the *American Can Company* and *Continental Can Company*. The association has established well-equipped laboratories in Washington, D.C., under the control of a scientific research committee. An important feature of the work of the laboratories is that the discoveries made are not intended to be confined to individual members of the association, but are also available to packers outside the organisation. This policy is adopted because it is believed that the effect of unsatisfactory packing on the part of a small or inexperienced firm may be detrimental to larger and more successful firms.

PLATE 32.—Electrical Laboratory for Photometry, Pennsylvania Railroad Company.

PLATE 33.—Lamp Testing Laboratory, Pennsylvania Railroad Company.

PLATE 34.—Heat Insulation Laboratory, Pennsylvania Railroad Company.

The laboratory comprises sections devoted to bacteriological and biological investigations, special work in connection with the examination of evaporated and condensed milk, one for general chemical analysis, and one specially devoted to the study of the action of foods on metal containers. In addition there is a full cannery equipment, where any canning operation can be so carried out under actual commercial conditions that exact data may be secured for further scientific investigation.

The laboratory buildings are rented, and the cost of equipment is approximately 4,000*l*. The annual maintenance expenses are between 6,000*l*. and 7,000*l*. in the laboratory itself, but in addition a great deal of investigation is carried out in the laboratories of individual firms connected with the association, and much of the materials used in the research laboratory are supplied by them.

A great deal of the recent work of the laboratory has involved the study of the weight of coating best adapted for the manufacture of plate intended for packers' cans, and the main part of the expense of this investigation is borne directly by can and tin-plate manufacturers.

A certain amount of commercial work connected with food technology is undertaken for individual members of the association, for which a fee sufficient to defray the actual cost of the investigation is charged. Where the work is undertaken for firms who do not support the laboratory a somewhat higher charge is made. It is found that this commercial work is of considerable value in bringing the laboratory into close relationship with the work of the canners.

It is generally felt by the leaders of the canning industry that the results of the laboratory investigations in solving some of the difficulties that in the past have caused imperfections in the packing of food will increase the sale of canned foods, with consequent advantage to the packers.

There appears among such associations to be the nucleus of a movement that may spread, and eventually become an important factor in placing industrial research on a national basis.

V.—UNIVERSITIES AND COLLEGES.

Some of the universities in the United States are maintained by private endowments, others partly from the proceeds of the land grants* and partly from a tax on the rateable property in the State. In the latter cases it might be expected that research resources would be directed mainly to industrial interests from which the financial support is derived. A careful consideration, however, of the conditions in the six States having the greatest manufacturing output fails to show, other than in isolated instances, very close co-ordination between university research and the manufacturing interests. On the other hand, in other States in which agriculture is more predominant definite efforts appear to be made to utilise the research facilities of the universities and colleges in the interests of the local industries.

---

* Under the Morrell Act each State was entrusted with land scrip of 30,000 acres for each senator and representative then in Congress, and the revenue from the sale of this land was to be utilised for the endowment of at least one college. The institutions thus endowed are known as "Land Grant Colleges."

Apart from Government institutions, the universities and colleges conduct the greatest amount of pure science research. In addition there is also a considerable amount of research that is applicable directly to industry. The work of the universities in these respects may be classified as follows :—

(a) That done by Students in connection with their Graduating Theses.

For this purpose a great deal of research is carried on in practically all the universities and technical colleges ; it is essentially of an educational character.

(b) Pure Science Research by the Staff.

This research is often of a very high order, and is carried out by the teaching staff in their spare time, the results being published usually in the scientific press or university journals.

(c) Research by the Staff for Private Firms.

This research is generally directed to the solution of some specific industrial problem, and carried out at the expense of the firm for whom it is done. In most cases the results are not published. Sometimes the problem may be of such a character that the college authorities are prepared to carry out the investigations free of cost, reserving the right to publish the results.

(d) Research in Experiment Stations.

In some cases research having a definite industrial objective is undertaken by a staff who devote their entire time to this work. In other cases it has to be undertaken conjointly with the regular educational work.

The following brief particulars are given of the most striking features of the research activities of a few of the universities and colleges.

VI.—EXAMPLES OF UNIVERSITY RESEARCH.

Clark University, Worcester, Mass.

At this university the department dealing with research is entirely independent, having its own appropriations, to be used as the director sees fit. All researches are carried out by graduate students who are candidates for the doctorate, and those problems are chosen which are suitable to the required thesis. These researches are published in the scientific press, such as the American Physical Review or the proceedings of the American Academy of Arts and Sciences. Some of the more recent problems dealt with include—

> Thermo-elastic relation in steel in the region of recalescence.
> An experimental study of transient induced currents in cylindrical cores.
> Experiments on a new dynamical method for the study of elastic hysteresis.
> Sound distortion in the telephone transmitter and receiver.
> The acoustic repulsion of jets of gas.

PLATE 35.—General Chemical Laboratory, Pennsylvania Railroad Company.

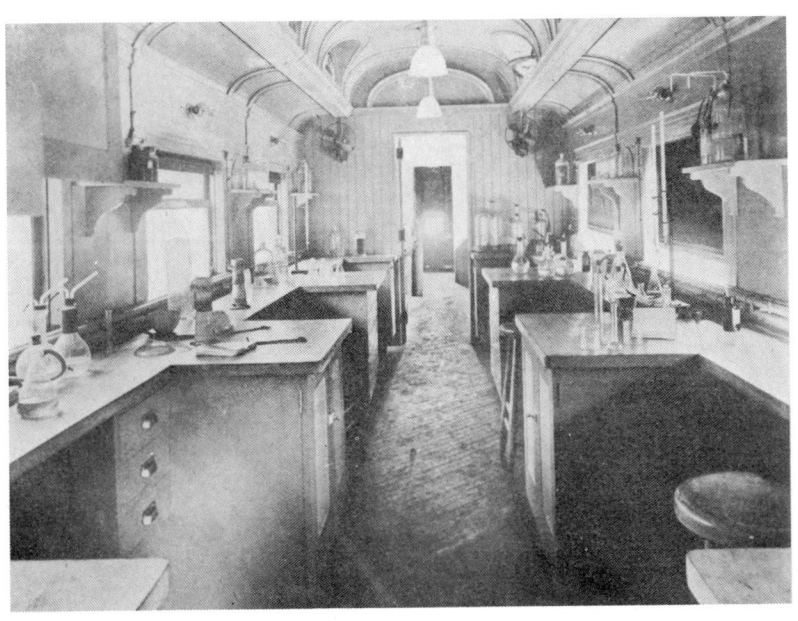

PLATE 36.—Laboratory Car, Pennsylvania Railroad Company.

PLATE 37.—Dynamometer Car, Pennsylvania Railroad Company.

PLATE 38.—Brake Shoe Testing Laboratory, Pennsylvania Railroad Company.

The problems selected may or may not have direct value in industry. The choice depends to a large extent on the student, and as a rule, whatever the character of the work may be, no restrictions are imposed as regards patents. Each student has a room to himself and the use of machine shop and of materials free. He is required to take such mathematical work or other subjects as will fit him for his particular study. These subjects are taught by the professors directing the research.

Columbia University, New York, N.Y.

Research is greatly encouraged in this university, and a great deal of very valuable work has been done by the staff, and by post-graduate students in preparation for their doctorate. These researches comprise those relating to building materials in connection with the departments of water supply, gas, and electricity of the city of New York; internal combustion engines; the manufacture of toluol and benzol by improved processes; wireless telegraphy and telephony; metallurgy; utilisation of forest products. It is held by the university authorities that through the medium of research much closer contact can be brought about between the university and industrial interests. In view of the extensive laboratory equipment of many of the large corporations and the demand made generally by industry for applied research, it has been considered that similar facilities established in connection with the university would be welcomed by those industrial concerns that are unable to maintain laboratories and staff for dealing with their problems. Proposals have been made to establish a research laboratory in connection with the university estimated to cost about 100,000*l.* with an equipment of about 30,000*l.*, and it is suggested that a fund for extension and endowment of from 400,000*l.* to 1,000,000*l.* would be required for this purpose. In connection with such a laboratory there would be developed a special technical library, the business of which would be to collect, compile, and classify in a manner to make it most available all information bearing upon the special problems to be investigated. The general proposals for such a laboratory have been outlined in the report for 1915 of the Dean of the School of Mines, Engineering, and Chemistry.

Cornell University, Ithaca, N.Y.

At this university there is a separate experiment station in connection with the Sibley College of Mechanical Engineering and the Mechanic Arts. Its staff comprises one professor, one assistant professor, and one instructor, all of whom give their entire time to research. The investigations are largely those of students doing special research problems, and in some cases special work is carried on by the staff. The laboratories and apparatus of the Sibley College are available for the staff of this experiment station when not in use for undergraduate work. Thus far the research department has not been very liberally supplied with funds, and no very extensive facilities are available for such work. At the same time, a good many important researches have been carried out, both by the graduates and the staff.

Harvard University, Cambridge, Mass.

The Massachusetts Institute of Technology is now incorporated in this university, and constitutes its School of Engineering. The electrical department of this institute has an experimental station devoted almost entirely to research work. It has at present an annual endowment of approximately 2,000l. for engineering research. The work is controlled by an executive committee, and the director and staff of the research department devote most of their time to the work of the station. No purely industrial researches are at present undertaken. There are ten research assistants, who are doctors, masters, or bachelors of engineering, and mostly graduates of the institute.

The researches carried out and published deal with such matters as the analysis of diaphragm vibrations, telephone receivers, skin effect in steel rails and other conductors at high frequencies.

The research men hold monthly meetings and discuss the progress of the various investigations, most of which are carried out with a view to preparing men for industrial careers. The work is of very great educational value, both to the research students and staff. Some research work is done before graduation, and if the student continues at the institute after obtaining his bachelor's degree he may become a paid assistant for a year or two before going into industrial life. Many of the men thus trained proceed to the technical laboratories of the United States Government.

Illinois State University, Urbana, Ill.

Much research work has been carried out in the various departments of this university, both by students for their graduating theses and by the staff, in connection with pure science problems and at the request of manufacturing firms. By far the most important research work, however, is that carried out by the engineering experiment station, which is one of the most important and successful of the engineering experiment stations attached to various universities in the United States. It was organised in 1903 for the purpose of conducting investigations of importance to professional engineers and to the manufacturing, railway, mining, and building interests of the State. A factor in the establishment of this station was the success that attended the agricultural experiment station at the same university, and it was thought that with the demand that existed in the States for scientific experimentation relating to manufacturing processes its establishment was justified. Its control is vested in the heads of the nine departments of the college of engineering, and these, with the director of the station, determine the character of the research to be undertaken.

The regular equipment of the laboratories of the engineering college is used for these investigations, but a permanent staff of nine investigators, each having the rank either of professor or assistant professor, is devoted entirely to research work, and has no educational responsibilities. In addition to this staff there are 14 research fellows, mostly from other universities, who are granted fellowships tenable for two years of the value of 100l. per annum each. These fellows spend half their time in research work, and the other half in preparation for the degree of M.Sc. The students of the university do not, as a rule, take part in the research work of the

PLATE 39.—Experimental Motor Testing Laboratory, Reo Motor Car Company.

PLATE 40.—Chemical Laboratory, T. A. Edison Laboratories.

PLATE 41.—Interior of Chemical Laboratory, T. A. Edison Laboratories.

PLATE 42.—Chemical Laboratory, Westinghouse Electric and Manufacturing Company.

station, but the spirit of research is fostered among them by the example of this work.

Work for private firms is not done by the experiment station, and all results are published. The bulletins are widely distributed free of cost in a large number of cases, and otherwise at a very low rate.

Among the bulletins that have been published are those relating to investigations on—

>   Ferro-concrete structures.
>   Locomotive problems.
>   Illinois coal.
>   Boiler construction.
>   Train resistance.
>   Magnetic properties of alloys.
>   Chemical investigations.
>   Boiler losses.
>   Wind stresses and steel frames of buildings, etc.

Altogether over 80 bulletins have now been issued, and they rank amongst the most authoritative work on the subjects concerned.

At the present time the cost of maintaining the experiment station is about 10,000$l.$ per annum.

In many instances industrial firms have co-operated with the experiment station, notably the Illinois Central Railway.

An important section of the engineering college is that devoted to ceramics. This department was commenced six or seven years ago, but has been considerably developed during the past three years. Its inception appears to have been due to a marked need by the ceramic industry in the State for men of scientific training. The course in ceramic engineering, as in other engineering departments, covers four years, of which the first two are common to all engineering work, and the last two specifically devoted to ceramics.

Apart from the work of the experiment station, very important investigations have been made by the students under the supervision of the staff of the electrical, mechanical, mining, and railway departments.

The following illustrations indicate the manner in which the various engineering laboratories are turned to account by the staff of the experiment station :—

Plate 53 illustrates a railway dynamometer car which is owned jointly by the University of Illinois and the Illinois Central Railway. It is equipped with apparatus for measuring and recording automatically draw-bar pull, speed, distance, locality, time, brake cylinder pressure, wind velocity, wind direction, and the temperature of one of the car journals. The car weighs about 31 tons, and can measure and record tractive force up to a maximum of 90,000 pounds. It is used in particular for train-resistance determinations and for economy tests of locomotives. It has been operated over the entire Illinois Central Railway system, also on the lines of the Baltimore and Ohio, New York Central, and New Jersey Central Railways.

Plate 54 shows the interior of this car.

Plate 55 shows the locomotive laboratory for investigations of locomotive machinery worked through its entire range of capacity while the locomotive remains stationary.

Plate 56 shows an electric railway test car fully equipped with all necessary recording devices.

Plate 57 illustrates refrigerating apparatus, and also apparatus for studying the effect of wind velocity and humidity on heat transmission through building materials, a pillar of which is shown in the foreground.

Plate 58 shows a portion of the equipment for conducting researches in connection with high quality magnetic steel produced under vacuum. The researches recently carried out with this apparatus are likely to be of enormous importance to the electrical industry. With their help iron rods are stated to have been produced having seven times the magnetic permeability of the best iron previously obtainable.

Plate 59 shows apparatus for research in connection with air washing plant.

Plate 60 shows a new form of electrical transmission dynamometer, in which the power transmitted is measured by the torsion of steel coupling rods, causing a displacement in the relative position of the fields of two alternating-current machines mechanically connected together. The voltage obtained by the armature of the two machines in series is proportional to the speed and the torque and is thus proportional to the power. This form of dynamometer is to be used in connection with various researches involving the measurement of power.

Plate 61 shows a drill press with dynamometer adjustments for investigations in connection with power consumption of such machines.

Iowa State College, Ames, Iowa.

At this college there is an engineering experiment station provided with a definite appropriation for experimental work amounting to about 5,000l. annually, of which 2,000l. must be expended on road investigations.

The experiment station staff comprises experts in civil, mechanical, electrical, mining, chemical, ceramic, and highway engineering, and in bacteriology and economic science. Most of these men devote their entire time to the work of the station.

The experimental work undertaken is confined principally to scientific investigations that will directly benefit the people of the State, both in connection with agriculture and manufacturing industries.

These researches cover a wide range of subjects. A few of the most important are investigations relating to Iowa fire clays, theory of loads on pipes in ditches, loads in culverts, sewage-disposal plants, ice-making, rust-resisting properties of drainage materials, Iowa coal studies, and the insulation of kilns.

University of Kansas, Lawrence, Kan.

In 1908 an engineering experiment station was organised in connection with the engineering school of the university. This has now a staff of nine men from the various departments of engineering. This research staff is relieved to some extent of teaching duties.

PLATE 43.—Physical Laboratory, Westinghouse Company.

PLATE 44.—Magnetic Laboratory, Westinghouse Company.

PLATE 45.—High Tension Laboratory, Westinghouse Company.

PLATE 46.—Moulded Insulation Laboratory, Westinghouse Company.

Thus far a number of useful bulletins have been issued, and several researches are in progress.

The equipment of the engineering laboratories is available for the use of the staff of the experiment station. Up to the present the research output has not been very extensive, but earnest efforts are being made to employ the facilities of the experiment station for the benefit of the various industries of the State. For this purpose statistics were obtained of the existing condition of these industries in order to determine in what manner the university could best co-operate. These data were prepared for such industries as cement, glass, leather, shoe manufacture, zinc smelting, straw board and paper mills, foundry machine shops, soda ash plant and cotton materials.

The chemical research bureau of the university, which is closely allied with the school of engineering, deals with problems distinctly chemical in their nature, and up to the present has issued some bulletins dealing with water purification and sewage disposal. This bureau is related to mining engineering, and has done a considerable amount of work in connection with flotation methods for the separation of zinc ores. In the school of engineering bulletins have been issued relating to researches connected with fuel supplies, municipal water supplies, etc.

The annual expenditure in chemical and engineering research is about 1,500*l*.

Lehigh University, South Bethlehem, Pa.

This university has no regular department for industrial research, but in the department of mining some important investigations have been done relating to oil flotation and mining matters. In the department of civil engineering a good deal of research has been carried out relating to reinforced concrete columns and other structural material. An interesting investigation also is that now proceeding in connection with ageing of a 3-inch steel cable in use in Cuba, portions of which are sent annually to the university to be tested for physical properties.

University of Michigan, Ann Arbor, Mich.

A notable feature in connection with the research work of this university is the testing tank for marine architecture. The work done there has been an important factor in the development of the freight boats for lake traffic, which have to be of shallow draft, small in the beam, of considerable carrying capacity, and running with very little wash. This testing tank is said to be the only one of its kind available for public work in the States. A considerable amount of research work is done by post-graduate men, and some of the local industries, notably Messrs. Dodge Bros., automobile manufacturers, and the Detroit Edison Company, as already noted, together with certain scientific societies, maintain fellowships there valued at 100*l*. each for one year. The holders of these fellowships devote their time largely to research investigations. In addition to research work of this character, a number of the local manufacturers have had machine tools and other apparatus experimentally investigated at the university for improvements in design.

Ohio State University, Columbus, O.

In addition to the regular post-graduate work of the students and the pure science investigations by the staff, a certain amount of research work is done for local industries, and an experiment station is just now being established. In this university, as in the case of Illinois State University, there is a department for ceramic engineering. It is expected that a considerable amount of pure science research will be dealt with in the experiment station now being organised.

Princeton University, N.J.

The Palmer Physical Laboratory of this university is one of the most up-to-date and best equipped laboratories in the country, and in it a great deal of research work is carried on. Each research student has a room to himself, and works under the supervision of professors, who devote part of their time to teaching. Some co-operation exists between the university and industrial concerns, particularly in electrical engineering.

Worcester Polytechnic Institute, Worcester, Mass.

A number of students of this college, after obtaining their B.Sc. degree, proceed to the professional degree of electrical engineer or mechanical engineer. This ordinarily involves one year of resident graduate work and the presentation of an acceptable thesis. One large engineering firm selects about four men each year from the graduate class to pursue certain research work for that company in the course of a period of two years, of which one half is spent in research and the other half in preparation for the professional degree. At the end of the two-year period these students enter the company's research department. They also spend their vacations at the works. A sum is provided through the head of the engineering department for the maintenance of these selected students.

The investigations at present being carried out by these students include :— dielectric losses in materials ; calibration of the sphere spark gap ; arcing under oil in connection with circuit breakers, oil switches, etc. The real function of these researches is educational rather than the acquisition of results of special scientific value.

A considerable amount of investigation has been done in street traction by means of an electrical testing car which is very fully equipped for this purpose. Plate 62 shows the interior of this car. Plate 63 shows the same car arranged for performance tests in the laboratory stand.

Land Grant Colleges.

There are at present about 15 of the Land Grant Colleges having experiment stations for research work. In most cases, however, these are staffed by professors and instructors who have to carry on teaching work in addition to research.

Other Colleges.

Apart from the colleges mentioned, a good deal of research is carried on in other universities and State colleges, as for instance at the University of Wisconsin,

PLATE 47.—Vapour Converter Research employing Works Equipment, Westinghouse Company.

PLATE 48.—Flywheel Investigations in Works, Westinghouse Company.

PLATE 49.—New Research Building in course of construction, Westinghouse Company.

PLATE 50.—Circuit Laboratory, Western Electric Company.

which has associated with it the Forest Products Laboratory of the Department of Agriculture. At Yale University co-operation exists with local firms in carrying out researches connected with their products, more especially in physics and metallurgical work. At Cornell University a good many research investigations of an industrial character are carried out, one of these of considerable importance being that dealing with the hydration of Portland cement, made at the instigation of the Raymond Cement Pile Company. This company provided fellowships necessary for the investigation. At Purdue University—apart from other research—an important investigation was carried out in conjunction with the Railway Association in regard to simultaneous methods of braking large freight trains.

While much of the research of the American universities is on the same general lines as that in similar institutions in the United Kingdom, special mention must be made of the engineering experiment stations. In these institutions the research staff is entirely or mainly distinct from the educational staff. The stations connected with the Illinois State University and the Massachusetts Institute of Technology have already been described, and in one or two other universities experiment stations have been or are in process of being established.

The practice followed by a number of firms and scientific societies of endowing fellowships at the universities is important, and likely to constitute a very beneficial link between the universities and industry. The plan at the Worcester Polytechnic Institute, Yale, and other colleges, by which research men are selected and trained in the interests of certain industrial firms, who provide a maintenance allowance, is a further indication of the interest taken by manufacturers in research work.

The existence of large research laboratories connected with individual corporations must have a considerable influence in inducing students to follow a post-graduate course, including a training in research, with a view to securing interesting and remunerative employment in such laboratories.

It is interesting to note the means taken by some research laboratories, such as the Engineering Experiment Station of the Illinois State University, to publish and distribute widely the results of investigations of the greatest importance in industry. A further interesting feature is that, while undergraduates are not generally allowed to take part in the research work, the proximity of men of eminence, such as are employed on investigations of great importance in many such laboratories, cannot fail to be a source of considerable inspiration to the younger men.

VII.—MELLON INSTITUTE OF INDUSTRIAL RESEARCH AND SCHOOL OF SPECIFIC INDUSTRIES.

This institute is associated with the University of Pittsburg, and is quite unique in its organisation and object. It was founded in order to provide manufacturers with the services of a great scientific laboratory and trained staff for the investigation of problems arising in their industry at an expenditure far less than would be involved in the establishment of their own private laboratories. Manufacturers are encouraged to submit their problems, and when these involve research, are required to endow fellowships for a period of one or more years for as many men as are needed to undertake the investigation. They also pay for such special apparatus and material as may be required and the travelling expenses of the research fellow.

The buildings, equipment, and endowment for the maintenance of a permanent staff were provided by the Mellon Brothers, bankers, of Pittsburg. The buildings cost approximately 50,000*l*., and the equipment 16,000*l*. Plate 64 shows a general view of the institute. The work of the research fellows is supervised by a permanent staff, which includes seven men of high scientific standing. When a specific research is to be conducted, the director of the institute undertakes to secure the services of a suitable investigator, usually from one of the universities, and in a most cases this is a man possessing a doctor's degree. Great care is taken in the selection to ensure that the candidate is inherently fitted to co-operate with the men engaged in the industry to which the research applies. If the problem is intimately connected with the works, the research fellow usually spends some time in the industry in order to become acquainted with the working conditions, and then carries out investigations in the institute, or partly there and partly in the works as the conditions may require.

The salaries paid to the research fellows are determined mutually by the director of the institute and the manufacturer and themselves. In a number of instances bonuses have been paid in addition to the pre-arranged salaries. The salaries vary from about 100*l*. to 400*l*. per annum. The total amount spent annually in salaries and maintenance of the institute is upwards of 30,000*l*.

The institute buildings are equipped with upwards of 30 laboratories provided with complete facilities for chemical and physical testing. Some of these laboratories provide accommodation for two workers such as that illustrated in Plate 65. Other laboratories provide for only one worker, such as that shown in Plate 66.

When a research is nearing successful completion in the laboratory it is usual to erect a unit plant on a small manufacturing scale in order to develop the process fully before it is attempted on a commercial scale in the works. Plate 67 is an illustration of such a plant.

This plan of working has been in operation for the past five years, during which time 75 research fellows have been appointed. There are at present 65 fellows working in connection with the laboratory and 36 researches are in progress. The full capacity of the institute is for 70 workers.

The investigations carried out thus far cover a wide variety of problems and include those dealing with crude petroleum, baking, aluminium, glue, soap, glass, yeast, leather, fertilisers, ores, copper leaching and acetylene.

The results of researches are not published until three years after their completion except by consent of the manufacturer, and may be deferred for a longer period than this if it can reasonably be shown that publication would be inimical to his interests.

Apart from the unique character of this institution and the facilities it affords for industrial investigations to be carried out at the minimum cost a most interesting feature is the fact that manufacturers at the conclusion of a research are usually

PLATE 51.—Telephone Instrument Laboratory, Western Electric Company.

PLATE 52.—Transmission Branch Laboratory, Western Electric Company.

PLATE 53.—Railway Dynamometer Car, University of Illinois.

PLATE 54.—Interior of Dynamometer Car, University of Illinois.

anxious to secure the services of the research fellow, and thus the highest positions in industries tend to become filled by men of sound scientific value. Another important feature is the extremely wide range of industries that have made use of the institute, which has had considerable educational value in focussing the attention of industrial people on the advantages of research.

In almost all cases the researches have been successful and many have resulted in considerable financial returns to the industry concerned.

In selecting research men the director considers that personality and common sense are all-important. He realises that in the application of science in industry the human element is of much greater importance than in the case of pure science research, where the experimenter does not come into contact with men in industry, who often are not in sympathy with scientific investigation. Up to the present a great deal of the work of the institute has been of a chemical nature, and most of the research fellows have been trained as chemists. In their work in the institute they are divided into groups, and assisted and supervised by one of the permanent staff.

Apart from the work of these investigators the permanent staff have their own laboratories and carry on their own researches, the results of which are published from time to time in the technical press. One hundred papers have been published up to the present, the subjects of a few of which are as follows:—

Some problems in copper leaching.
Smoke and industrial nuisance.
Smoke problems of the manufacturer.
The relation of nitrogen to humus in arid grounds.
Cracking of petroleum.
Fluorescence of petroleum distillates.
The optical activity of petroleum and its significance.
The use of iodine as a dehydrating and condensing agent.
The function of enzymes in bread.
Radio-active matter in geology.
Radio-active matter in the atmosphere.
Some colloidal solutions derived from hydrated alumina.

VIII.—NATIONAL INSTITUTIONS.

The most important national institutions dealing with industrial research are:— the Bureau of Standards, the Carnegie Institution,[*] the Smithsonian Institution,[*] the Department of Agriculture, the Forest Products Laboratory, the Bureau of Mines.

The Department of Agriculture and Bureau of Mines, while only indirectly connected with manufacture, are worthy of consideration in that they embody organisations that might serve as a basis for industrial research in connection with manufacture on a national scale.

---

[*] It may be noted that these institutions were founded and endowed by private individuals, but are undoubtedly doing national work. The Carnegie Institution is governed by a Board of Trustees, and the Smithsonian Institution by a Board of Regents.

Bureau of Standards, Washington, D.C.

The function of this institution is to deal with standards of length, time and mass, standards of quality, specifications of materials, standards of performance and determination of physical constants. A great deal of work has also been done in connection with the standardisation of railway transportation charges, telephone service and safety codes.

The bureau comprises laboratories for physical, chemical, electrical and engineering work, and includes four buildings, 200 feet long, 55 to 60 feet wide, and four stories high, together with three or four smaller buildings for special work. The plans for extension include two more large buildings. Plate 68 shows a general view of the bureau, Plate 69 the engineering building, Plate 70 the electrical building.

The large buildings cost about 50,000*l*. each to erect, and in all the cost of buildings and ground amounts to 200,000*l*., and the equipment about one-third of that sum. The annual maintenance cost is about 120,000*l*. An auxiliary laboratory is established in Pittsburg for the testing and investigation of the more common structural materials met with in that industrial centre.

The work of the bureau is subdivided as follows :—

(a) *Weights and Measures,* including standards of mass, length, time, volume, and density, the testing of measuring instruments for Government service, and the preparation of standards for industrial purposes.

(b) *Thermometry, pyrometry and heat measurements,* including temperature of measuring standards of all kinds, the investigation of the radiating properties of metals and oxides, the testing of refractory materials, gas calorimetry, thermal conductivities of materials, refrigerating work.

(c) *Electricity,* including various electrical standards, the testing of electrical instruments, magnetic testing, photometry, illuminating engineering, electrolysis, radio-telegraphy and telephony.

(d) *Optics,* including spectroscopic studies, polarimetry in connection with sugar testing, colour standards and specifications, photographic investigations and lenses.

(e) *Chemistry,* including methods of chemical investigations regarding the ferrous and non-ferrous alloys, analysis of coal, chemistry of papers, lubricating oils, rubber, soap, paint, gas analysis, bituminous materials, ceramics, textiles and drugs, engineering research and testing in connection with aerodynamics, petrol machines and vacuum apparatus.

(f) *Metallurgy,* dealing with bronzes, rare metals, failure of rail apparatus, ingot investigations, failure of structural brasses, distribution of carbon in steels and irons and investigations of moulding sands.

(g) *Structural Engineering and miscellaneous materials,* including tests on structural steel columns for buildings and bridges, behaviour of spring steel under various conditions of stress, Portland cement investigations and vitrification of clays.

PLATE 55.—Locomotive Testing Laboratory, University of Illinois.

PLATE 56.—Electric Test Car, University of Illinois.

PLATE 57.—Apparatus for Special Research, University of Illinois.

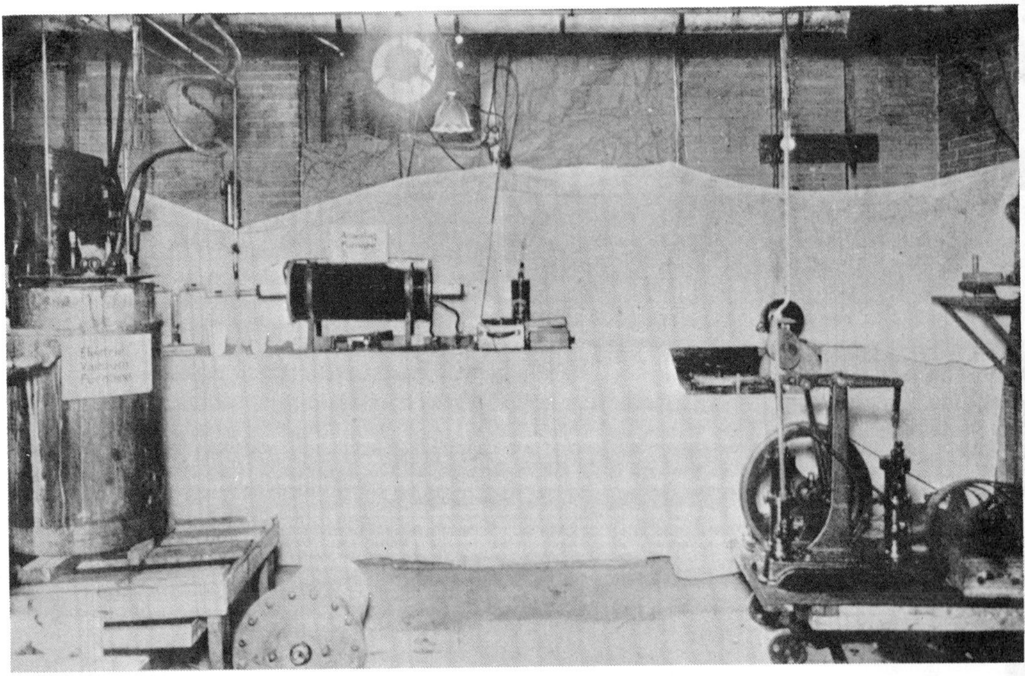

PLATE 58.—Apparatus for Special Magnetic Research, University of Illinois.

A great deal of work is carried out in connection with the testing requirements of various Government departments, such as those pertaining to the Navy, public health, weather bureau, treasury, etc., and specifications have been established for the purchase of materials and the testing of contractors' supplies, carried out particularly in the case of materials such as cements, paints, oils, papers, etc. In connection with these investigations model plants are available for the manufacture of paper, rubber products, cement mixing and ceramics.

Very cordial co-operation exists between the bureau and the industries, and manufacturers' plant is sometimes utilised for full-scale experimental processes. Numerous requests for information are received from individual manufacturers, national, state, and municipal laboratories, scientific investigators, committees on engineering, and technical societies. These inquiries comprise a wide variety of subjects, such as those relating to thermometry, pyrometers, optical instruments, melting points of materials, flash-point tests, design of aeroplanes, non-magnetic and non-expansible alloys, metallographic methods and temperature control in the manufacture of ordnance.

A considerable amount of special work has been undertaken in connection with colour standards, particularly in regard to such commercial materials as oils, papers, textiles, silks and dyes. Advice is given freely, but where special investigation is necessary which has not a common application to the requirements of a considerable section of the public, a charge is made to cover the expense thus incurred. Where it can be shown, however, that the research is likely to lead to the benefit of a large number of people, the work may be carried out at the public expense. For instance, at the request of a body of refrigerating machine manufacturers, a research extending over a period of five years was made to determine the physical constants used in that industry. This research involved an expenditure of about 3,000$l.$ per annum, and was carried out at the public expense.

Apart from co-operation with individual manufacturers, a great deal of research work has been accomplished in conjunction with manufacturers' associations, such, for instance, as the American Society of Refrigerating Engineers, National Electric Light Association, Pennsylvania Railroad Company, National Dairy Union, Association of American Portland Cement Manufacturers, Associated Metal Lath Manufacturers, Gypsum Industries Association, National Lime Manufacturers' Association, Hollow Tile Manufacturers' Association, American Refractory Association, National Brick Manufacturers' Association, General Cotton Manufacturers' Association, and Underwriters' Laboratory.

Similar co-operation exists with the prominent technical societies, such as the American Gas Institute, Automobile Club, American Chemical Society, American Society for Testing Materials, American Institute of Metals, American Society of Civil Engineers, American Railway Engineering Society.

A good deal of investigation has been done in co-operation with public utility companies, such as those relating to electric light, gas, street, railway, and telephones, which has included scientific and engineering research, the preparation of specifications regarding quality of service, methods of testing, and safety rules.

The laboratory equipment of the bureau is very complete. Plate 71 shows facilities for physical testing on a large scale by means of the Emery testing machine, which has a capacity of 2,500,000 lbs. in compression and about half that in tension. Plate 72 and Plate 73 show various structures, which were prepared in conjunction with industrial concerns, undergoing tests.

Extensive facilities are available for producing and investigating on a full manufacturing scale papers, rubber products, cements and ceramics. Plate 74, for instance, shows an experimental cement kiln.

The bureau does not carry on such routine testing work as can ordinarily be done by private commercial laboratories.

The present staff numbers upwards of 400, of whom about 75 per cent. have had scientific and technical training.

Information is issued regularly by the bureau in the following forms :—
 (a) Papers dealing with purely scientific investigations prepared by the staff.
 (b) Technological papers giving the results of investigations, often arising from problems presented by manufacturers.
 (c) Circulars of information of a popular character embodying not only the work of the bureau, but also technical data of educational and scientific character for the general enlightenment of the public.

There is a growing tendency for manufacturers to bring their problems to the bureau for solution, and often even firms having large research laboratories make use of the facilities thus offered. The bureau may in this way ultimately serve as a means of linking up research facilities throughout the United States. Already the bureau has carried on what really amounts to important educational work by teaching the value of scientific investigation in place of rule-of-thumb methods, and this has resulted in many cases in the establishment by manufacturers of their own research laboratories.

Carnegie Institution, Washington, D.C.

This institution was founded in 1902, and has at present an endowment fund of approximately 4,500,000*l.*, yielding an annual interest of 5 per cent. of this amount. The articles of incorporation of the institution declare " That the objects of " the corporation shall be to encourage in the broadest and most liberal manner " investigation, research, and discovery, and the application of knowledge to the " improvement of mankind." The general organisation has been planned to secure these objects, involving—
 (1) The formation of departments of research within the institution itself to attack problems requiring the collaboration of several investigators, special equipment and continuous effort.
 (2) The provision of means whereby individuals may undertake and carry on to completion investigations not less important, but requiring less collaboration and less special equipment.
 (3) The publication of the results of research.

PLATE 59.—Air Washing Plant, University of Illinois.

PLATE 60.—Electric Dynamometer developed for Research, University of Illinois.

PLATE 61.—Dynamometer Investigations on Machine Tools, University of Illinois.

The various departments of the institution comprise those relating to experimental evolution; botanical research; embryology; marine biology; terrestrial magnetism, etc. Laboratories in connection with these and other fields of investigation have been set up in various parts of the States. An idea of the scale on which the laboratories are planned may be judged from Plate 75, showing the geophysical laboratory, and from Plate 76, showing the laboratory for terrestrial magnetism. A non-magnetic ship of sea-going capacity has also been constructed for carrying out various investigations in connection with terrestrial magnetism. There are also departments for research in history, economics, and sociology. A number of investigators in colleges and universities are assisted by the institution in connection with work not directed to the acquisition of academic degrees.

Smithsonian Institution.

This institution carries on a certain amount of research work, which, however, is not to any great extent directly applicable in industry. It assists, by small money grants, investigators of various universities and colleges by defraying to some extent the expenses of scientific researches. It also undertakes the publication of a certain amount of scientific literature.

Department of Agriculture.

This department is subdivided into a number of sections dealing respectively with weather, animal and plant industries, chemistry, soils, experiment stations, forest service, biological survey, entomology and roads. From an industrial point of view the most interesting sections are those of the experiment stations and forest service.

There are a large number of experiment stations in various parts of the country, and these are supported mainly by the individual States, and partly by funds from the Federal Government. The direct management of the stations is largely in the hands of the officers of each State.

In addition to the investigations at the laboratory at the headquarters in Washington, each experiment station carries on investigations pertaining to local agricultural needs. Such investigations include, for instance, the study of the improvement of wheat by hybridisation and the effect of environmental influence on the chemical composition of wheat; *animal husbandry*, including the investigation of the heat production from rations fed to animals in a respiration calorimeter, the most efficient foods for animals, and the effect of in-breeding; *poultry investigations*, including the effect of cross-breeding, the influence of various foods on yield of eggs, and a study of the bacterial content of eggs; *dairying*, including the study of milk production in relation to quality and character of food, germ content of milk, pigmentation, and the effect of various food diets; *rural economy*, including the economic aspects of farming, economic size, and proportion of tilled to dairy land; *entomological research*, comprising methods of destroying insects in grain, fruit, animals, trees, etc.; *horticultural investigations*, comprising a study of the best method of tillage, chemical study of fruits, plant diseases, including the investigation of cereals, fruit trees, etc., and methods of dealing with known diseases; *soil investigations*, embodying studies of the physics, chemistry, and bacteriology of the soils.

In addition to the investigations of the experiment stations a number of experimental farms are worked in different localities, and demonstrations and lectures provided.

A large number of bulletins are issued, of which there are two principal kinds. One of these deals with matters of interest to local agriculturists, couched in simple terms and understandable by all; the other is of a more technical character, better adapted to those who have had an agricultural college training. Numerous inquiries are received from every part of the States, which are answered individually from the experiment stations or the Government department.

Forest Products Laboratory, Madison, Wis.

This laboratory is associated with the Forest Service Section of the Department of Agriculture. It was established in 1910, and has the co-operation of the University of Wisconsin to the extent of being provided therefrom with buildings, heat, light and power. The laboratory building, an illustration of which is shown in Plate 77, was erected at a cost of approximately 10,000*l.*, and the maintenance, heat, light and power, etc., cost annually about 1,200*l.* The laboratory equipment cost upwards of 20,000*l.*, and the Government makes an annual appropriation of about 28,000*l.* for upkeep. The staff numbers between 80 and 90, of whom about 40 have had scientific training as chemical engineers, engineers, physicists and foresters. The aim of the laboratory is to promote economy and efficiency in the utilisation of wood and in the processes by which forest materials are converted into commercial products. In carrying this out the purpose is—

(*a*) To secure authoritative information of the mechanical and physical properties of the commercial woods and products secured from them.

(*b*) To study and develop the fundamental principles underlying the seasoning and kiln drying of wood, its preservation and use for the production of wood pulp, paper, etc., and in the manufacture of alcohol, turpentine, resin, tar, and other chemical products.

(*c*) To develop practical ways and means of using wood which under present conditions is being wasted.

(*d*) To co-operate with consumers of forest products in improving present methods of use, in formulating specifications and grading rules for commercial woods and materials secured from them, and in making the information secured available to the public through bulletins, correspondence, and other means.

It is the policy of the laboratory to secure to a large extent the co-operation of the wood-using industries. As a rule no investigation conducted by the laboratory is considered complete until the results obtained experimentally have been checked on a commercial scale in the industrial application department. This is usually accomplished through co-operation with individuals or companies using wood products, particularly in the case of paper-making. Plate 78 shows the laboratory for wood

PLATE 62.—Electric Test Car, Interior, Worcester Polytechnic Institute.

PLATE 63.—Electric Test Car, Worcester Polytechnic Institute.

PLATE 64.—Mellon Institute of Industrial Research.

PLATE 65.—Laboratory for two Research Fellows, Mellon Institute.

preservation. Plate 79 illustrates the paper-making plant installed in the laboratory. Plate 80 shows the apparatus for the production of ethylalcohol from waste timber.

Formerly the investigations of the laboratory were all published in Government bulletins. This practice has given way to publication in trade and scientific journals until the more complete or exhaustive monographs are issued by the departments.

The work of the laboratory is carried out on very extensive lines, and the facilities it affords are widely used by people interested in the use of forest products. Anyone is at liberty to correspond with the laboratory in regard to problems dealing with the use of wood, and information on such matters is furnished free. The laboratory also acts in a consulting capacity to men in charge of the handling and sale of timber, and also to those who require data as to the physical properties of timber employed in constructional work.

Bureau of Mines.

This bureau was commenced about five years ago, and has for its object the safeguarding of the health and interests of workers in the mining industries, and the improvement of efficiency and prevention of waste in preparing and utilising mineral resources. It is entirely a non-partisan organisation, and seeks the co-operation of all interested parties, including workmen's organisations, technical societies, state officials and state governments. Before the establishment of the bureau a great deal of work was carried on in connection with fuel-testing under the supervision of the United States Geological Survey, and its work ultimately culminated in the establishment of an experiment station in Pittsburg for testing mining explosives.

The main divisions of the bureau are the following :—

Mining, which includes field investigations of mining methods in coal and metals, instructions as regards rescue and safety work, inspection, explosives, chemical tests, and electrical inspection.

Metallurgical, dealing with smelter fumes, hydrometallurgy of lead and zinc, working of low-grade complex ores, steel manufacture and corrosion of metals.

Mineral technology, which includes rare metal investigations, this work being done largely in co-operation with the National Radium Institute ; the study of tungsten ores, platinum resources, molybdenum deposits, non-ferrous alloys, ceramic materials, abrasives and paints.

Fuels and mechanical equipment, testing of coal and fuel, sampling and analysis, physical and chemical tests, spontaneous combustion, and briquetting.

Petroleum and natural gases, production, transportation, storage, refining, and inspection of petroleum-bearing lands.

Chemical research laboratory. This links up the various other divisions, and deals specifically with the origin of coals, physical tests, chemical tests, analysis of samples, volatile products, clinkering tests and gases.

The present headquarters are situated in temporary premises at Pittsburg. Plans are prepared and the authorities are proceeding with a new building near the University of Pittsburg. The buildings will comprise mechanical laboratory, chemical laboratory, metallurgical and fuel-testing laboratories, boiler house, lecture theatre, and other offices and laboratories. At present there is an appropriation of 100,000*l.* for dealing with the buildings at present planned. It is considered that the present plan will have to be considerably extended in the near future.

In addition to these headquarters it is intended to maintain 10 mining experiment stations and 7 mine-safety stations in connection with the most important mining districts. It is anticipated that the sum necessary for extending investigations and providing equipment and carrying on the work for the year 1917 will be about 75,000*l.*

Large-scale researches have been carried out in order to ascertain the cause and to find a remedy for and prevention of gaseous and dust explosions.

In connection with petroleum investigations, a great deal of work has been done to reduce the enormous losses in the production of oil and gas, and to bring about less wasteful methods in the recovery of such materials. Methods have also been developed for extending the use of gas and oil for fuel and other purposes, for obtaining larger proportions of gasoline from petroleum, and for producing such compounds as benzol and toluol.

New legislation has been introduced to secure the reduction of accidents among ore dressers and in smelting plants, and the direct prevention of accidents by suitable preventives devised as a result of investigations of the bureau.

Valuable savings have been effected by the proper check of quality and the purchase by specification of Government coal. By-products of an estimated value of 8,000,000*l.* per annum have been recovered from coke-making plants by the development of new industries, including the manufacture of dyestuffs and coal tar derivatives.

In co-operation with the American Institute of Metals and the Chemical Department of Cornell University a careful study was made of brass and non-ferrous alloy manufacture, and methods determined for the prevention of metal losses.

In co-operation with the National Radium Institute a great deal of valuable work has been done and national resources conserved by carrying out refinements in extraction of radium previously done abroad.

From careful investigations of drilling methods in oil and gas wells a process was devised by which a vast amount of waste previously incurred was saved.

In other directions investigations attended by a great deal of success have been made to prevent damage by smelter smoke. Special investigations have also been undertaken in connection with the treatment of low-grade and complex ores, and in the leaching of gold and silver ores.

The bureau publishes three classes of reports, namely, bulletins, technical papers, and miners' circulars. The bulletins present in detail the results of technical and scientific investigations, and are mainly of interest to engineers, chemists, and mine officials. The technical papers are less formal than the bulletins, and the miners' circulars deal with such topics as those relating to accident prevention.

PLATE 66.—Laboratory for one Research Fellow, Mellon Institute.

PLATE 67.—Example of Unit Research Plant, Mellon Institute.

PLATE 68.—General View, Bureau of Standards.

PLATE 69.—Engineering Building, Bureau of Standards.

IX.—COMMERCIAL RESEARCH LABORATORIES.

There are a considerable number of commercial research laboratories in the most important industrial centres. Of these the following may be cited as examples :—

The Institute of Industrial Research, Washington, D.C.

This institute, an illustration of which is shown in Plate 81, employs about a dozen technologists. According to the articles of incorporation, the objects of the institute are to investigate and improve processes of manufacture ; to co-operate with manufacturers in the reduction of costs, and in the utilisation of by-products ; to investigate and improve general metallurgical, mining, and agricultural operations ; to disseminate information in regard to such improvements ; to study the problems of paint technology, electrical engineering and electro-chemistry ; to institute economies and improvements in the manufacture of fertilisers and general chemicals ; to train and instruct graduates of scientific and technical schools and other persons in industrial research, and to aid them in obtaining work for which they are particularly fitted. The laboratory appears to be very well equipped for the purposes for which it is intended, and special attention is given to researches in metallurgy, paint technology, food and agricultural chemistry, drugs and materials of construction, subdivisions of the laboratory being arranged for these purposes. Outdoor proving grounds are available for testing the effects of atmospheric corrosion on paints and metals.

The laboratory was established in 1910, and its services are in demand by many industrial concerns. A number of bulletins are issued describing some of the researches carried out by the institute, which include—

The preservation of the exterior of wooden buildings.
The sanitary value of wall paints.
Paints for cypress and their necessity.
The effect of colour upon the durability of paint.
Certified analysis of bitumen in wood and paving materials of highway engineers and contractors.
Notes on the study of the temperature gradients of setting Portland cement.
Bitumen roads and pavements and their materials of construction.
Conservation and its relation to pharmaceutical chemistry.

In addition to the above, a number of scattered papers prepared by the staff have been published in the technical press.

Electrical Testing Laboratories, New York, N.Y.

A general view of these laboratories is shown in Plate 82. The establishment is controlled by the bond-holders connected with the association of Edison Illuminating Companies. The laboratories were organised in 1900 with a staff of six, which has now increased to 125. The total floor area of the buildings is approximately 30,000 sq. ft.

The primary object of the laboratories is lamp-testing, about twenty million being tested annually. In addition to the very extensive facilities for such work in New York, a large staff of experts is maintained in various lamp factories and in other electrical manufacturing concerns to carry out routine tests, only refined decision tests being referred to headquarters. Plate 83 shows one section of the laboratory for lamp-testing.

In addition to this work, a variety of other investigations is undertaken, largely of an electrical character, although there is also a good deal of such work as physical tests on specimens; chemical tests and analyses; photomicrographic work; fuel-testing; oils, lubricants and paper.

A number of small laboratories are also provided in the main laboratory building, which can be rented to private individuals desiring to carry out their own line of research. An illustration of one of these is shown in Plate 84. The organisation comprises laboratories for magnetic, electrical, chemical, mechanical, photometric and high-voltage investigations, and also a well equipped machine shop. While only a small part of the work of the laboratories is of a purely research character, some excellent work has been done along these lines, and in general this laboratory is among the most important of the commercial undertakings of its kind.

Fitzgerald Laboratories, Inc., Niagara Falls, N.Y.

The development of the Niagara Falls region has resulted in enormous industrial expansion, and these laboratories were founded in response to the need for some means of investigating manufacturing problems arising from it. Manufacturers in difficulties were encouraged to seek a solution through the laboratory, the larger part of the work of which appears to relate to the electric furnace, and its commercial development in the manufacture of steel, zinc, abrasives, etc. Plate 85 shows a corner of the furnace laboratory.

Detroit Testing Laboratories, Detroit, Mich.

This laboratory is a purely commercial undertaking, and a great deal of its work includes investigations in dairy problems, and those connected with oil, grease, and soap manufacture and use. It also carries out investigations in road building, concrete construction, water, sewage and sanitation research, and the perfection of manufacturing methods for industrial concerns.

The laboratory is equipped with departments for metallurgical and physical testing, fuel testing, food, water, bacteriological investigations, and industrial and chemical research.

The staff numbers 16 in all.

Pittsburg Testing Laboratory, Pittsburg, Pa.

This is a private laboratory established in 1881 as a commercial institution for making chemical analyses, physical tests and inspection of materials of construction. In addition, a great deal of research and industrial investigational work

PLATE 70.—Electrical Building, Bureau of Standards.

PLATE 71.—Physical Testing Machine, Bureau of Standards.

PLATE 72.—Tests on Masonry Pillar, Bureau of Standards.

has been carried out in connection with ceramic industries, especially glass and enamel. Also in oil refining, condensation processes and the development of manganese from waste products.

The laboratory comprises a five-story building, and a separate two-story building for research on a semi-manufacturing scale. In addition to a staff of several hundred inspectors, about 20 chemists are employed partly on analytical, partly on research work.

The value of buildings and equipment is about 10,000*l*.

The results of a number of the researches carried out have been published in the technical press.

Laboratory of A. D. Little, Inc., Boston, Mass.

This firm of chemists and engineers maintains extensive facilities for chemical, metallurgical, and physical testing; also a model mill for industrial research in paper-making, as well as other full-scale manufacturing equipment. The staff of the laboratory is about 75, of whom rather more than half are technical graduates. The firm acts in a consulting capacity in connection with all industrial research problems. A notable example is that of the work at present being undertaken by Mr. Little on behalf of the Canadian Pacific Railway, the scope of which is to determine and investigate the natural resources and materials available throughout the district served by the railway; to determine the best and most economical utilisation of these materials; to design plant for carrying out the manufacturing processes thus involved; to standardise the products manufactured, and assist in finding a market for them. The materials to be dealt with comprise mineral deposits, coal, oil, timber and agricultural products and probably many other natural products that at present are unknown.

In addition to work of this character the firm investigates various problems arising in connection with textile, chemical, and cellulose products, and reports are frequently prepared for the benefit of financiers in addition to those relating to the scientific problems involved.

A further most important movement in which Mr. Little has participated has been the preparation of a new course in chemical engineering connected with the Massachusetts Institute of Technology. This matter is of such importance, and the plan proposed so comprehensive, that a brief outline may be of general interest, particularly as it has very marked bearing on industrial research in connection with the chemical industry.

The proposal is to establish a number—probably seven—of chemical engineering and research stations at carefully selected industrial centres. The equipment of each station will comprise a fireproof building, containing lecture room, laboratory for routine chemical work, and a special research laboratory with offices for staff and a carefully selected library. The cost of each building would probably be about 5,000*l*., and its equipment from 2,000*l*. to 3,000*l*. The centres selected for the stations are Boston, Pittsburg, Chicago, Rumford Falls (Maine), Niagara Falls, N.Y., Bayonne, N.J., and the Lehigh Valley.

The experiment stations in these centres would deal severally with gas industry, iron, steel, coke, glass, tinplate work, soap, fertilisers, glue, wood pulp and paper, general chemical manufacture, petroleum distillation and manufacture of Portland cement. In order to deal with specialised lines of chemical manufacture, including dyes, it is suggested that a further station be installed at the headquarters of the institute. The total cost of erecting and equipping these stations would be probably under 100,000*l*., and the cost of maintenance about 12,000*l*. per annum.

The total length of course in chemical engineering would be five years, of which the first three would be spent in the newly erected buildings of the Massachusetts Institute of Technology. At the end of the third year selected students would be sent to the chemical engineering stations, spending six weeks in each, and the last year would again be spent at the headquarters of the institute.

In view of the fact that hardly any suitable means are available at present for systematic preparation for chemical engineering, the progress of this scheme, if carried into effect, will be watched with very great interest.*

Wahl-Henius Institute of Fermentology, Chicago.

This institute was established in 1886 as a scientific station for brewing. While one of its principal functions now is to provide courses of instruction in brewing, malting, bottling, and general brewery engineering, it also serves as a consulting bureau for the brewing industry, provides specialists for inspecting breweries and experts in every branch, and also carries out a considerable amount of research work in connection with fermentation processes.

The institute is equipped completely for carrying out every process required in the brewing industry on a commercial scale, and has very complete laboratories for research work, comprising sections for chemical analysis and bacteriology. A great many of the researches carried out have been published in the scientific and trade press.

There are a number of other testing laboratories operating on commercial lines in various cities in the States, but in general they are not of any great importance, and are concerned as a rule with routine testing rather than research investigations.

X.—SCIENTIFIC SOCIETIES.

The proceedings of the scientific societies as well as the technical press offer channels for making public the results of valuable researches by individual workers. A notable example is the United Engineering Society, comprising the Institutions of Mining, Mechanical, and Electrical Engineers. Some of the scientific societies are interested in or control endowment funds for research work.

In connection with the Society of Automobile Engineers there is a standards committee having a research division. This division is composed almost entirely

---

* The most recent information available shows that a five-year course has been put into operation. All students taking Chemical Engineering pursue the same course until the end of the third year. During the fourth year, students proceeding to the Master's degree spend six weeks at each of five experiment stations at Bangor, Me., Everett, Mass., Niagara Falls, N.Y., Stamford, Conn., and Northampton, Pa.

PLATE 73.—Tests on Lattice Girder, Bureau of Standards.

PLATE 74.—Experimental Cement Kiln, Bureau of Standards.

PLATE 75.—Geophysical Laboratory, Carnegie Institution.

of college professors having laboratories at their disposal, in which work of interest to the society is from time to time carried out. Research reports of various manufacturers connected with the automobile industry are frequently made available to the different divisions of the Standards Committee. There is, however, no research carried out directly by the society, nor has it any funds for this purpose.

The American Society for Testing Materials has a most important influence in industry by determining the best methods of testing and the correct specifications to use for the purchase of materials. The membership of the society is very influential and comprises not only many of the most prominent engineers and chemists, but also the leading manufacturing firms. The preparation of specifications of materials is carried out by committees consisting of representatives of users and makers of materials relating, in the main, to engineering. A great deal of research work is carried out in this connection by member-firms. The Pennsylvania Railroad Company, whose research facilities have already been described, has carried out a great many of these investigations.

XI.—ENDOWMENTS FOR SCIENTIFIC RESEARCH.

Apart from the numerous endowments made to various universities and colleges, some of which may be employed specifically for research, and which generally impose conditions as to residence or studentship at the institution to which the endowment applies, there are a number of funds that have been established for scientific research without such obligations. Some of the most important of these are the following :—

> The Carnegie Institution Endowment Fund of approximately 4,500,000*l*., the administration of which has already been described.
>
> The Hodgkins Fund of 50,000*l*., administered by the Smithsonian Institution.
>
> The Ambrose Swasey Fund of 40,000*l*., administered under the direction of the Engineering Endowment Fund.
>
> The Colburn Fund of 15,000*l*., and General Research Fund of 5,000*l*., administered by the American Association for the Advancement of Science.
>
> The Bache Fund of 11,000*l*., the Wolcott Fund of 1,100*l*., the Comstock Fund of 2,400*l*., and the Draper Fund of 2,000*l*., administered by the National Academy of Sciences.
>
> The Rumford Fund of 13,500*l*., and the C. M. Warren Fund of 2,500*l*. administered by the American Academy of Arts and Sciences.
>
> The Elizabeth Thompson Science Fund of 5,200*l*.
>
> The California Academy of Sciences administers endowments yielding about 14,000*l*. annually, a part of which is devoted to research.

Numerous endowment funds have also been provided in connection with medical, astronomical, and other research.

XII.—CO-ORDINATION OF RESEARCH IN THE UNITED STATES.

The institutions that have been described are only a part of those by means of which research is promoted in the United States. All of them are the product of quite recent years; and collectively they form a trial on a gigantic scale of the application of science to modern industry. The success of this application is shown by industrial results such as those which have been quoted; and the deep conviction among American business men of its value to their industries is evident from the unceasing additions which are being made to their existing facilities for industrial research.

As yet little has been done to prevent overlapping, by which the resources of several institutions may be absorbed on the same problem, which is solved no more completely by all of them than it is by any one. Still less is there at present any comprehensive scheme of research applying to industry in the United States as a whole, and only in such interests as agriculture, and in a lesser degree mining, is research organised on anything approaching national lines. On the other hand, the development of extensive laboratory facilities in manufacturing corporations, universities, and Government institutions demands and must tend inevitably to some form of co-ordination, so as to avoid wasteful overlapping. This may eventually lead to the nationalisation of research in industry.*

An important influence in this direction is the growing appreciation of the possibilities of export markets and the need to combine manufacturing facilities in order to meet international competition effectively. At present the lack of legislative unity in the different States, a vast home market, and the keen competition between firms in the same industries, have retarded such a national movement.

In President Wilson's Address to Congress, delivered December 7th, 1915, suggestions were embodied for mobilising economic resources, and the necessity was urged of affording Federal aid to industrial and vocational education, as had long been done in the agricultural industry. Prior to this announcement a movement was started by the Land Grant College Engineering Association, which has resulted in the promotion of a Bill for "Mechanic Arts Experimentation," now known as the Newlands Bill (No. 4874). This Bill has for its object to establish under the direction of the Land Grant College in each State a department to be known as the "Mechanic Arts Experiment Station," for the purpose of conducting original researches, verifying experiments, and compiling data in the mechanic arts and in their application to improving the conditions of the rural and industrial classes in the United States; also for conducting researches, investigations, and experiments in the production, extraction, and manufacture of substances utilised

---

* Since the above was written, a National Research Council has been appointed by the National Academy of Sciences at the request of President Wilson. The Council has already had placed at its disposal the resources of the Engineering Foundation, a body originally established to further scientific and engineering research, and working under the auspices of the four principal engineering societies. It thus becomes possessed of a permanent secretary and funds. The members of the Council include the most prominent research men in the States, and all departments of research are represented. The object in view is to co-ordinate the scientific research work of the country in order to secure efficiency in the solution of the problems of war and peace.

PLATE 76.—Laboratory for Terrestrial Magnetism, Carnegie Institution.

PLATE 77.—Forest Products Laboratory.

PLATE 78.—Wood Preservation Plant, Forest Products Laboratory.

in the application of mechanic arts to industrial pursuits, and such other researches or experiments bearing directly on the various industries of the States as may in each case be deemed advisable, having due regard to the varying conditions and needs of the representative States.

To carry out the requirements of the proposed Bill the Federal Government is asked to appropriate a sum of approximately 3,000*l*. per annum to each State, and one Government department is designated as co-ordinator to act in the same relation to the proposed Mechanic Arts Experiment Station as that now existing between the Department of Agriculture and the Agricultural Experiment Stations in the various States. It is proposed that these experiment stations should co-operate with the Agricultural Experiment Stations in solving engineering problems that are intimately related to the industry of agriculture, such as flood protection, drainage, farm sanitation, irrigation, and road building. The opinion expressed by a large number of scientific men and technologists indicates strong support for the Bill, which is considered likely to be very beneficial to national industry, and to disclose much latent scientific talent in the country.

Another movement, having for its object the more effective adaptation of research facilities in the various universities and experiment stations to industrial and national needs, has been started by the American Association for the Advancement of Science, which has appointed a Committee of One Hundred to deal with the matter, comprising some of the most prominent research men connected with industry. This committee is at present investigating means of selecting and training research students, the condition of research in educational institutions, and a means of stimulating appreciation of industrial research. It is also compiling data of endowments and grants available for research.*

In another direction the urgent need that is felt for an organisation to prevent overlapping of research is expressed in a letter of February 15th, 1916, by Dr. A. E. Kennelly, published in the Journal of the Franklin Institute, March 1916. This communication suggests that the Franklin Institute might co-ordinate the efforts of the various universities, give fuller publicity to the research work in hand, offer grants to laboratories, and encourage interest and co-operation between industries and the universities.

The appointment of the Naval Advisory Board for dealing with the naval engineering problems has resulted in the proposal to provide a very extensive research laboratory, and to turn to wider account in some way the resources of universities and manufacturing laboratories. It is suggested that a Government official attached to the proposed laboratory might serve as a link between industrial problems and national research facilities, and advise the lines on which co-operation might be effected.

---

* The Sub-Committee on Research in Industrial Laboratories presented at a meeting of the Committee of One Hundred on Scientific Research a report covering the organisation of industrial research, the selection and training of students, and the necessity for co-operation between manufacturers and Universities and between manufacturers and research institutions. This report, presented by Dr. R. F. Bacon, the chairman of the Sub-Committee, and printed in Science, N.S., Vol. XLV., No. 1150, pages 34–39, Jan. 12th, 1917, is a valuable and illuminating document, and should be read by all interested in industrial research. *See also* Dr. C. E. K. Mees (a member of the Sub-Committee), in Science, N.S., Vol. XLIII., No. 1118, pages 763–773, and Dr. Bacon, in the Journal of the Society of Chemical Industry, Vol. 35, No. 1, 1916.

As already noted, the Department of Agriculture and the Bureau of Mines represent very complete organisations for dealing with their own particular fields of research, and embody some features and much experience which might serve as a basis for a national research scheme in any other industry. Particularly is this so in regard to the means that have been developed by these two Government departments for collecting and distributing data to those to whom it is of value.

XIII.—SELECTION AND TRAINING OF RESEARCH MEN.

Scientific and technical research, which has done so much to make the industrial fortune of Germany, has now been introduced into the commercial equipment of the United States, and it is little more than a rhetorical question to ask whether this country can afford to dispense with an advantage which has already proved so fruitful in the hands of its most intelligent and powerful competitors. A condition precedent to working any general system or systems of industrial research in a country where relatively little systematic individual research has been done up to now is to provide the men by whom researches are to be made.

The selection and training of men for research depends to some extent on the character of the investigations to be undertaken, and the experience which has just been described throws some light on possible methods.

The chief points in the methods of selection used in the United States may for convenience be shortly re-stated. In large laboratories, in which the staff is expected to undertake work in pure science, the tendency has been to select from the universities men who have had a thorough education in mathematics and physics, and preferably those who have taken a doctor's degree. Where the research has been of a more applied character, technical graduates have been employed largely, with or without a preliminary experience in works; and, as has been noted above, many men who have established reputations as experimenters, either in universities or such national institutions as the Bureau of Standards, have been absorbed in the United States by industrial concerns, as they would be, and in isolated cases already have been, in this country. This expectation is confirmed by the experience already described of the Mellon Institute, where the research fellows, though selected mainly from the universities, have been chosen very largely for their ability to co-operate with men in industry, and have repeatedly found their own way into responsible industrial positions.

The excellent scheme already referred to as in operation at the Worcester Polytechnic Institute, by which selected graduates are specially trained in research for a large firm, which contributes to their maintenance, has been successful in American practice, and is likely to be useful in this country.

The training of the younger men has an essential bearing on the work which is done in research institutions. The juniors have virtually to continue their training under the guidance of the senior research staff, much as is done, for instance, at the Mellon Institute; and for this purpose it is very desirable that a good deal of pure science investigation should be carried on, since this keeps the staff fully in touch with the most modern developments, and gives interest to their work. Where possible, also, the results of these special investigations are and should be made public.

PLATE 79.—Paper Making Plant, Forest Products Laboratory.

PLATE 80.—Chemical By-Products Plant, Forest Products Laboratory.

PLATE 81.—Institute of Industrial Research, Washington.

PLATE 82.—Electrical Testing Laboratories, New York.

It is sometimes considered that an investigator who has specialised on pure science research does not readily adapt himself to investigations of a more industrial character. The experience of at least one large research laboratory in the United States shows that this is by no means the case.

The American practice in regard to remuneration may also be considered in view of its satisfactory results. In the Bureau of Standards, and also in some of the large private research laboratories, definite grades of employment are established, the lower ones being essentially devoted to preparing men for the higher posts.

The salaries paid to research men—usually college graduates—in junior positions in the large industrial and State laboratories, generally commence at about 150*l*. to 200*l*. per annum, and rise in the course of four or five years to about 400*l*. per annum. The higher positions are paid on a correspondingly higher scale. In the Mellon Institute, as already noted, the remuneration is fixed by special arrangement according to the character of the investigations.

American experience suggests also a possible arrangement for training research workers in this country. The men might be selected from graduates in the universities, who could proceed straight into research laboratories—such as the central national laboratory referred to later—or alternatively spend the first year or two in post-graduate work at the university. A promising plan is that adopted by one large British engineering firm, which is prepared to employ selected graduates and provide them with some works' experience for a period long enough to acquaint them with urgent industrial problems. Having then selected a subject for research, and while the student is still in the employ of the company, the investigation can be undertaken either at the works or at the university, whichever offers the most suitable facilities. In this way the student has an excellent opportunity of undertaking work of immediate industrial value, and moreover he is brought into close contact with the commercial atmosphere of the works, which is invaluable to the man who ultimately expects to take up an industrial position.

A great deal of the research work of this country has hitherto been done by men of outstanding genius, and largely on this account an impression prevails that important scientific investigations can only be made by such men, who should be allowed to pursue their course unhampered and undistracted by association with industry. While full credit should be given to the genius who can often achieve so much with very limited facilities, it is a fallacy to assume that research work of great value cannot be carried out by men of more average attainments. This is illustrated by the success achieved in many of the laboratories in the States, where, with suitable organisation, important investigations both directly connected with industry and in pure science have been successfully dealt with by men of no more than average ability working under competent direction.

Such an example is of no particular concern to the quality of the research work, but it is absolutely vital to the quantity, and to what in relation to quantity may properly be called the efficiency of the institutions which undertake research. To utilise our national research resources to the fullest extent it is necessary to turn to account the several capacities of all our men of scientific training, and to plan an organisation that will link up their efforts and direct the results of their investigations into the most productive channels.

XIV.—SOME FUNDAMENTAL CONSIDERATIONS.

In connection with industrial research the most vital considerations are the calibre of the scientific men and the characteristics of men in industry on whom the application of the results of research depends. As already noted, manufacturers in the United States excel in the aptitude for turning scientific discoveries to industrial account. Great Britain excels in the number and excellence of its physicists, but is not so fortunate in regard to the supply of men who patiently and persistently apply the discoveries of science to industry.

The commanding position held by all British industries a century ago has created a deeply rooted feeling of security among a large body of manufacturers, and this, together with a natural conservatism, militates against the ready adoption of new proposals such as extensive research in which the financial prospect is not assured. Again, in many cases the heads of British manufacturing industries of the present generation are not educated in a manner that gives them a keen appreciation of scientific knowledge. It is not fully realised that industrial conditions have changed, and that many of the conditions which originally enabled British industries to assume a premier position no longer exist. On the other hand, it is sometimes thought that British manufacturers possess a greater inherent capacity for organising labour and turning to account manufacturing facilities than any of their international competitors, and that this may to a considerable extent offset the advantages which the latter derive from organised scientific research. The position of an industry, however, is determined not so much by the capacity of manufacturers as by their performance; and moreover it must not be forgotten that while in certain industries, as for instance, those related to the motor-car and aviation, manufacturers in this country have overtaken their more progressive foreign rivals, the priority achieved by those who carry out the pioneer work yields a most important advantage.

Another important factor is the character of industrial markets. The manufacturers of the United States possess a vast home market, and thus far have given comparatively little attention to export work, so that the research facilities of different firms in the same industry have been utilised for competing between themselves. Some fears have been expressed that these extensive research facilities may prove a serious menace to competitive industries in this country. While this may well be the case if American manufacturers seriously organise themselves for capturing foreign markets, they are likely to be handicapped for some considerable time through the abnormal inflation of the wages of industrial workers during the past two years, which will not readily be readjusted. As against this, however, the wealth that has floated into the United States during that period may be conserved and applied to the reduction of indirect manufacturing expenses, the development of greatly improved labour-saving appliances, and the cheapening of transport facilities. The handicap of inflated wages, which may not be confined to the United States, will thus be enormously reduced in that country by the effects, direct and indirect, of the wealth that it has collected so rapidly.

PLATE 83.—Lamp Testing Laboratory, Electrical Testing Laboratories.

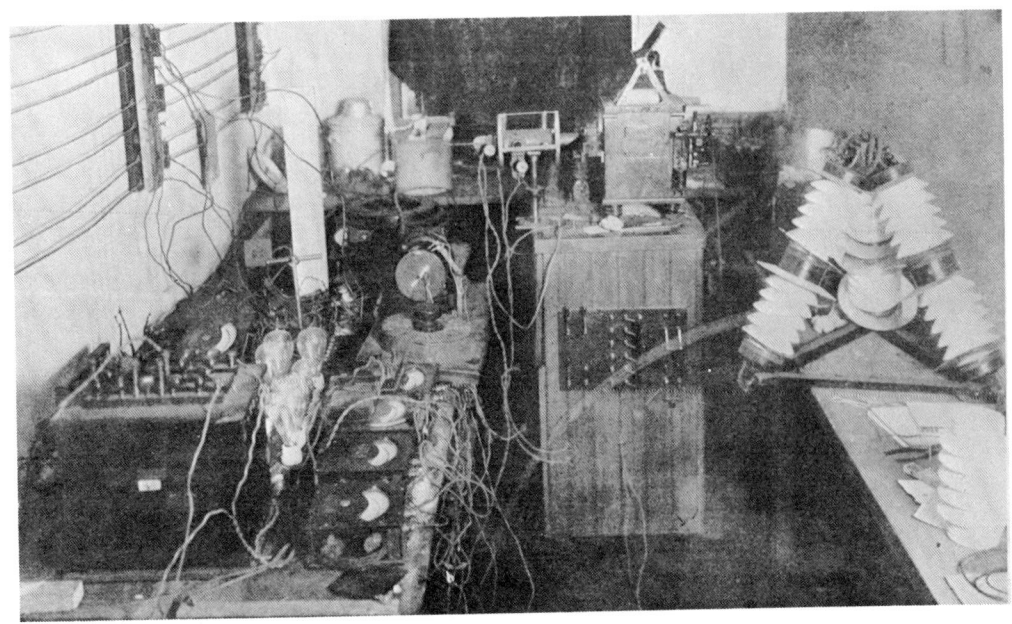

PLATE 84.—Private Research Laboratory, Electrical Testing Laboratories.

PLATE 85.—Corner of Furnace Laboratory, Fitzgerald Laboratories.

In this country, while there is a great deal of internal competition for home markets, international markets are of increasing importance, and from the point of view of research it is necessary to consider what are the best means of co-ordinating scientific resources in order to employ them most effectively against foreign competitors.

In every industry progress is the result of continual acquisition and application of new knowledge, and in a competitive market progress is indispensable to success. Competitors therefore are successful according to the extent to which they are able usefully to employ new knowledge as compared with their less progressive rivals. In ordinary circumstances and in the least highly developed and organised industries new knowledge is acquired by workers as a result of their everyday employment, or occasionally by men of genius, who are able almost instinctively to achieve discoveries having immediate application in industry. Such has been the history of many British industries, and the people of this country appear to possess in many respects an innate capacity for making progress by such means. As industries become more highly organised and manufacture is more subdivided and specialised, there is less opportunity for the individual worker to acquire new knowledge, and consequently investigation from which such knowledge is derived can only be carried out effectively by men devoted to that purpose who possess the necessary scientific education and training. Research facilities organised in this way cannot but be more effective than the older and more haphazard plan, and it is by adapting new methods to new conditions on these lines that the present marked progress in industrial research in the United States is proceeding.

The importance to an industry of contemporary research and progress in sciences and technical arts associated with other industries is often overlooked. For instance, mechanical flight was impossible until the successful development of the petrol motor. The construction of the Panama Canal was delayed until the discovery by Ross of means for successfully dealing with malaria. All industries are affected by research resulting in the improved health of the worker, or which brings about a better understanding of the conditions governing fatigue and consequent loss of efficiency, and by researches such as those of Taylor, often though they may have been misunderstood and misapplied, which deal with the elimination of wasteful physical effort in the everyday employment of industrial workers.

The fact that progress in various branches of science not bearing directly on industry may ultimately have far-reaching industrial benefits indicates the value of men trained in scientific research as compared with haphazard rule-of-thumb investigators, since the latter are not so likely or so able to observe and appreciate what falls outside their own line of work.

In the contemplation of any particular research, it is first of all important to ascertain what scientific work has already been accomplished along the same lines elsewhere. This necessitates the world-wide collection of scientific data. An important feature of this is made in the leading American research laboratories, as indicated by the extensive library facilities they employ. It is almost equally important that scientific data, prepared in a manner in which they can be most readily assimilated, should be distributed to industry and to all who can use the knowledge. Such dissemination of information is a difficult problem, and as industrial people are not yet sufficiently appreciative of the need for scientific knowledge, much valuable information now available is not utilised. This is notable in connection with the results published of the researches carried out in several of the colleges and experiment stations in the United States. Examples of the effective distribution of well-prepared literature are those afforded by the Department of Agriculture, Bureau of Standards, the experiment station of the Illinois State University, and other prominent institutions. It is worthy of note that in the States there is an increasing tendency to publish research work in current trade or scientific journals rather than to compile it in the form of a Journal with a limited circulation issued at comparatively rare intervals.

The application in industry of any scientific discovery resulting in a new product, or the improvement or cheapening of an existing commodity, ultimately reacts to the benefit of the community as a whole. For example, the researches in illumination that led to the discovery of the metal filament lamp resulted directly in benefit to the public through a reduction in the cost of domestic lighting, and nationally in the conservation of a considerable extent of one of the great natural resources, namely, coal. The investigations resulting in the successful fixation of atmospheric nitrogen have led to the artificial production of fertilisers and other valuable commodities. Many scientific researches have led to subsidiary discoveries, which result in a vast network of industries, such as those associated with coal tar products, dyes, explosives, etc. Such discoveries have often referred to unused or imperfectly used resources of individual neighbourhoods, and as a result of them very prosperous industries have grown up in certain localities, as for example, the vast chemical industries in the neighbourhood of Niagara Falls. The wealth produced by such industries re-acts to the benefit and prosperity of a whole country.

It may thus be argued that any research which has for its object the improvement of commodities or the development of new industries should receive public support. No section of the community remains unaffected by research : the capitalist, because by means of scientific discovery there may be opened up new and promising fields for investment and new means of safeguarding investments that he has already made ; the manufacturer, not only by the obvious advantage of facilitating his manufacturing processes, but because this asset enhances his standing and enables him the more readily to raise capital for his business ; the educationist, because research work opens up new fields for studies and demands new methods of training ; the artisan, because the more extensive the research work, the greater the probability of maintaining the lead in industry and the greater the ultimate national prosperity.

XV.—ORGANISATION OF BRITISH INDUSTRIAL RESEARCH.

The general considerations which have last been discussed may now be applied to the particular needs of the British Empire.

While there are prominent British manufacturers who appreciate the potentialities of industrial research, it must be conceded that as a body they consider such investigation to be an expensive luxury. On the other hand, during the past two years there has been disclosed in British industries an enormous latent capacity for adaptability to entirely new lines of manufacture, many of which have depended for their development upon scientific research. The research facilities, however, that have been created to such an extent during the past two years are as yet quite disproportionate to the magnitude of British industry, and it is highly desirable that the present awakening to the use of science should be fostered, and research facilities suitably organised.

For this purpose it is essential that any national scheme of research be designed on ideal lines to which existing organisation should be subordinated, so that in this way the development can proceed progressively until ultimately the plan is consummated.

From the standpoint of the individual firm, the most effective weapon in industrial competition is the application of new knowledge resulting from research applied to some immediate industrial problem. In pursuing an investigation, however, towards a definite goal, it is well known that many promising ramifications are often disclosed, which, when followed, lead to results that may be more valuable even than the original objective. In this way it may often happen that a research carried out in the interests of one industry may lead to results which prove invaluable if applied to some quite different industry. The higher forms of research, more especially those in the field of pure science, should therefore be carried out on national lines, so that any results that are derived can find application in one or other of the numerous national industries.

It is even more important that such research be organised on lines which will link up the scientific resources of the Empire. The work of the Institute of Science and Industry in Australia, and the research now being developed by the Canadian Pacific Railway, together with similar efforts that may be made in other parts of the Overseas Dominions, should be linked up with a national scheme in this country.* Apart from the interchange of scientific knowledge, such an Imperial scheme would assist the utilisation of raw materials, and in this way foster the development of the natural resources of the Empire. It is quite as important for manufacturers in Great Britain to interest themselves in any means which will improve and cheapen their raw material supplies, as it is to direct scientific methods to the cheapening of manufacturing processes. An Imperial research organisation might not only result in the development of means for cheapening the production of raw materials, but also, where new materials are discovered in the Overseas Dominions, assist in finding suitable outlets for their use.

* In the Australian scheme for a Commonwealth Institute of Science and Industry, each State has been requested to form a local Committee, and a census of existing research work is being taken, together with particulars of work required which will help local industries. Some researches have already been initiated in connection with mining and agriculture. Several of the Dominions are considering schemes for co-ordinating their work on similar lines.

An important consideration affecting industrial conditions after the War is that considerable manufacturing resources, comprising plant, machines, tools, and trained labour, will have accumulated, some of which may be turned to national benefit if they can be adapted to the manufacture of products hitherto obtained from abroad. In thus developing new lines of manufacture organised research may be of very considerable benefit. In order thus to meet international competition it is necessary to bring each manufacturing process to the highest degree of efficiency by the elimination of haphazard and wasteful methods.

With regard to the financial aspect of research, experience in the States shows that the efficiency of a well-organised laboratory increases considerably with its size, and moreover, only the large laboratories can employ methods of full-scale manufacture, which not only materially assist in the efficient development of new products, but also secure considerable revenue from the sale of commodities produced in this way. Thus the annual maintenance cost of the laboratory of the Eastman Kodak Company is 30,000*l.*, representing less than 1 per cent. of the annual profits of the company.

Viewing the American experience in the light of the considerations described above, the following seem to be the most important of the alternative schemes of research that might be employed in Great Britain :—

(*a*) Research laboratories in individual works.
(*b*) Research laboratories for a group of works in the same industry.
(*c*) The centralisation of research in the universities or colleges.
(*d*) An Imperial centralised laboratory for the whole of industry.

(a) Individual Works Laboratories.

The most effective way of conducting industrial research would be to equip each works with its own laboratory. By this means the most intimate needs of the firm could be studied and effectively dealt with, and such a close combination of works, organisation, and scientific investigation would probably result in a number of very efficiently conducted firms. It is clear, however, that only the largest works could support laboratories on an extensive scale. An enormous amount of overlapping would occur, since each laboratory in the same industry would probably carry on very similar work ; most firms could not stand the financial burden of such a laboratory ; there would be an insufficient number of really first-class research men available to staff such laboratories ; and it would hardly be practicable to carry out investigations of a purely scientific character, since the possibilities of turning a large part of the results of investigations to account in any one firm or industry would be comparatively small. Further, while by such means individual firms would be able to compete keenly with each other, their scientific resources would not be organised in the best way to meet competition in international markets.

Complete research laboratories in individual works only appear possible in the case of very large organisations, although, as noted later, individual laboratories adapted for dealing with immediate needs are highly desirable when operated in conjunction with a larger research scheme.

(b) Research Laboratories for a group of Works in the same Industry.

Different firms in the same industry employ very similar manufacturing facilities, and in order that the greatest possible improvement can be made in tools, methods, and processes, it is desirable that the various firms should pool for their common benefit all the experience and research facilities they possess that will assist this object. For this purpose a central laboratory might be arranged for each industry or for a group of similar firms in the same locality.

In those cases where firms have secret processes in connection with which investigations are required, these would be carried out by each firm on its own account. Many such processes, however, are of much less importance than is commonly supposed, and the experimental work thus involved would probably represent not more than a small portion of the total research requirements.

Such arrangements are already in vogue to a limited extent in this country; for instance, a central laboratory for research work is maintained in the Sheffield district, where two of the largest steel firms in intimate commercial alliance support a common research laboratory. In other cases facilities for common research have followed on the fusion of the commercial interests of two separate firms, as has occurred in the pottery district. While it may be argued that the pooling of resources may entail some self-sacrifice on the part of larger firms, from which their smaller competitors would benefit, this is probably not a very important matter, since many processes could for financial reasons only be taken advantage of by the largest firm. In any case, however, while such combinations might in the case of some firms involve a temporary loss, improvements arising from joint research would probably enable every firm to recoup far more than it expends, owing to the increased amount of business and greater working economy arising from the application of the discoveries made. The time was never so opportune for such co-operation, and never have competitive firms been so ready to share mutual interests.

(c) The Centralisation of Research in the Universities and Colleges.

The most extensive facilities for research in this country are at present possessed by the technical colleges and universities, and these are to some extent employed for dealing with miscellaneous investigations required by local industries. These facilities might be arranged so that each university served as a research station for one or other of the principal industries.

There are, however, many objections to this course. The function of the modern university is to educate, and its equipment and staff should be directed primarily to this end; the staff is not as a rule intimately in touch with industry, and the amount of research necessary for the industries of this country is far beyond all the resources of the universities. On the other hand, research is one of the finest possible means of educating young men for industrial employment, and consequently every encouragement should be given to graduates to pursue some research work under the guidance of an experienced experimentalist. For educational purposes the character of the research should be such as to develop the student's capacity to think for himself and increase his powers of observation and logical deduction.

At the present time, with the exception of the work of the National Physical Laboratory, most research in pure science is carried on in university laboratories, and such work is eminently suited to the capacity of the university staff. From the experience of the States it is clear that to be most effective in an industrial sense research investigations should be undertaken by a staff specially devoted to the purpose, and as far as possible also with equipment not required to be used for teaching purposes. In such cases there appears to be very little to be gained by attaching such special research laboratories or experiment stations to the universities. They might equally well be placed at other and possibly more convenient centres of industry.

(d) A centralised Imperial Research Laboratory for the whole of Industry.

The single laboratories dealing with the research requirements of each industry, such as outlined under (b), might all be grouped together in one centre—say the Midlands—and controlled by a board largely represented by manufacturers.

Such a combination would possess many advantages over separate laboratories. For instance, the cost of maintenance would be less, and through the common use of library, power supply, machine and other workshops, the first cost would also be lower. By far the greatest advantage, however, would be the benefits derived from the corporate life of such an institution, and the free interchange of experience and discussion of research work between the staffs of the various industrial sections. As already pointed out, in the pursuit of an investigation much new knowledge may be disclosed which has an important bearing on industries quite different from that of the original objective. In a laboratory confined to the needs of a single industry such new knowledge might be entirely lost, or if put on record might not come to the notice of those to whom it would be of the utmost benefit. In the centralised institution such a risk would be reduced. Further, such a laboratory would be best adapted for co-operating with the research institutions in the Overseas Dominions, and in fact would serve as a scientific focus for the whole Empire.

The staff of the laboratory would comprise a senior grade, representing the directors or heads of each industrial division; an intermediate grade, representing the principal body of research men; and the juniors, who would principally consist of graduates recently drawn from the universities. The senior staff would be permanent. The intermediate men would be continually migrating into industry as their value to manufacturers became appreciated, and this tendency would be encouraged so as gradually to permeate industry with well-trained scientific men. The junior staff would be permitted to employ part of their time in the laboratory in preparation for higher degrees, and in this way their appointment would be equivalent to a fellowship such as that tenable in some universities for post-graduate research, with the advantage that the training period would be spent under first-class research men, and the work undertaken would in most cases be of live industrial interest. The juniors would in course of time be promoted to the intermediate work.

In order to utilise every scientific asset the staff and facilities of the universities and of private research workers would be registered and incorporated as auxiliary to the central laboratory. The university staffs could from time to time for convenient periods take up research work in the central organisation itself, and in this manner keep closely in touch with modern progress.

While the function of the laboratory would be primarily to deal with problems confronting manufacturers, a considerable amount of original research in pure science would need to be done. On the other hand, the laboratory should be provided with means to carry on the actual manufacture of new products until this is undertaken by a regular commercial concern. While the first cost and the maintenance for some years would have to be provided out of public funds or by levy on the profits of industry, the institution ought to become self-supporting in time from the sale of products manufactured and from the licenses granted to manufacturers in connection with new or improved materials, processes, or tools.

Under present manufacturing conditions it frequently happens that the user of materials has to carry out the research necessary for their improvement. Fundamentally this practice is wrong, and such work should be carried out by the supplier. With the help of a centralised institution it would be possible for each branch of every industry to have its own research carried out there under the guidance of its governing body or trade association.

The importance of the collation of all scientific information, not only that pertaining to contemplated research, but also that of use in industry generally, has already been alluded to. The centralised organisation affords the best possible means of doing this, and also of disseminating it to those to whom it will be the greatest value. The laboratory would also issue bulletins of the work it carries out, and might also undertake the preparation of text-books in the most important and advanced branches of technology. The heads of the different sections of the laboratory would require to keep in close touch with the firms of the industry they represent, in order to carry out where necessary full-scale manufacturing experiments in works, and with the National Physical Laboratory, which would deal with all matters pertaining to standards and research connected therewith.

The establishment of such an organisation would tend to cause firms to instal their own laboratories in co-operation with the central laboratory for dealing scientifically with manufacturing troubles and special research problems incidental to their own products.

XVI.—CONCLUSIONS.

The most important conclusions that emerge from the above facts and considerations may be shortly stated.

Industry is the basis of national prosperity, and every resource should be used to facilitate its progress. The instances which have been given above show that in this respect research is of the utmost importance, and it must be regarded as an indispensable weapon wherewith to meet international competition. The success, however, of any comprehensive scheme of research depends largely upon the attitude of the manufacturers, and it is therefore of high national importance that they should not only appreciate the value of the application of science in industry, but also co-operate in assuring that it is applied systematically and sufficiently. Among the questions that arise immediately out of the need for industrial research is that of the education and training of men for all grades of industrial employment. The full benefits of scientific investigation will not be obtained unless the results are applied by suitably trained men. There is urgent need for consideration on national lines of means for the better education and training of youths who will be the future skilled workmen; and the demand expressed by many for a more important place for science in education needs no emphasis. It is not less necessary to give attention to the scientific training of those who proceed to the higher positions in industry from the universities, and particularly to impart to such students a thorough knowledge of the fundamentals of manufacturing economics. The development of research on a large scale, and the consequent possibilities of absorbing and lucrative employment, will tend to attract to the ranks of industry many of the ablest young men who nowadays enter non-productive professions. In this way their value from a national point of view will be immeasurably increased.

Though the investment involved in providing wide facilities for industrial research will be remunerative, and may be indispensable to the prosperity of individual industries and even of the nation itself, it must involve large sums of money, some part of which can bring no immediate result. Such measures cannot be introduced successfully unless they are supported by public opinion; and a great need therefore exists for bringing continually before the public the necessity of industrial research, with its possibilities and benefits. To this end the facilities afforded by the daily press, and particularly by the trade, technical, and scientific press, should be fully utilised, and further, these means might well afford channels not only for the distribution of information and knowledge to the general public, but for receiving from the latter suggestions and expressions of need for promising lines of investigation. In this manner public opinion may be developed along desirable lines and some latent scientific talent disclosed.

A new phase in industrial and economic life is commencing, and its development will be governed very largely by the extent to which new scientific knowledge is obtained and turned to the benefit of mankind. It is by the progressive use of research, every advance of which opens up ever wider industrial possibilities, by the fullest employment of the nation's inherent manufacturing capacity, and by the wise co-operation of labour and capital, that the prosperity of this country can be assured.

I desire to express my grateful thanks to the large number of American scientists connected with the various manufacturing corporations, universities, State and other scientific institutions referred to in this memorandum, not only for the personal facilities accorded to me when visiting their laboratories, but also for their courtesy in supplying me subsequently with much important information; also my indebtedness to the Management of the British Westinghouse Electric and Manufacturing Company for the permission—readily accorded—to make known the information thus obtained.

A. P. M. FLEMING.

August 22, 1916.

INDEX.

AGRICULTURE, connection of research work of universities with, 21, 24.
Agriculture, Department of, 28, 31, 35, 45, 50.
Aim of Memorandum, 1.
Ambrose Swasey Fund, 43.
American Academy of Arts and Sciences, 22, 43.
American Association for the Advancement of Science, 43, 45.
American Association of Woollen and Worsted Manufacturers, 20.
American Brass Company, Waterbury, Conn., 5.
American Can Company, 20.
American Chemical Society, 33.
American Gas Institute, 33.
American Institute of Metals, 33, 38.
American Locomotive Company, Schenectady, 18.
American Paper and Pulp Manufacturers' Association, 20.
American Physical Review, publication of researches in, 22.
American Rail Masters Mechanics Association, 15.
American Railway Engineering Society, 33.
American Refractory Association, 33.
American Rolling Mill Company, Middletown, O., 4.
American Society for Testing Materials, 4, 15, 33, 43.
American Society of Civil Engineers, 33.
American Society of Mechanical Engineers, 15.
American Society of Refrigerating Engineers, 33.
American Telephone and Telegraph Company, 18.
Associated Metal Lath Manufacturers, 20, 33.
Association of American Portland Cement Manufacturers, 20, 33.
Associations of Manufacturers, research work of, 2, 20–21, 33.
Australia: Commonwealth Institute of Science and Industry, 51.
Automobile Club, 33.
Automobile Engineers, Society of, 42.

BACHE FUND of the National Academy of Sciences, 43.

Bacon, Dr. R. F., reports by, 45.
Bausch and Lomb Optical Company, Rochester, N.Y., 18.
B. F. Goodrich Company, Akron, O., 10.
Brewing, Scientific Station for, 42.
British Industrial Research, organisation of, 50–55.
British Industries, past and present position of, 48.
Bureau of Mines, 6, 31, 37, 45.
Bureau of Standards, Washington, D.C., 15, 20, 31, 32–34, 46, 47, 50.

CALIFORNIA ACADEMY OF SCIENCES, research endowments of, 43.
Canadian Pacific Railway, research work on behalf of, 41, 51.
Carnegie Institution, Washington, D.C., 31, 34, 43.
Ceramic Engineering Departments at Universities, 25, 28.
Chemical Engineering, scheme for training in, 41.
Clark University, Worcester, Mass., 22.
C. M. Warren Fund of the American Academy of Arts and Sciences, 43.
Colburn Fund of the American Association for the Advancement of Science, 43.
Colleges, Land Grant, 21, 28, 44.
Colleges, research in, 2, 28–29.
Columbia University, New York, N.Y., 23.
Commercial objects, research applied to specific new, 3.
Commercial Research Laboratories, 2, 39–42.
Committee of One Hundred on Scientific Research, report of, 45.
Competition in Industry, 49, 56.
Comstock Fund of the National Academy of Sciences, 43.
Continental Can Company, 20.
Co-ordination of Research in the United States, 44–46.
Cornell University, Ithaca, N.Y., 23, 29, 38.
Cost of research in industrial laboratories, 7, 8, 15, 16, 18, 21, 41; in national institutions, 32, 36, 38; in universities and colleges, 23, 25, 27, 30.

DEPARTMENT OF AGRICULTURE, 28, 31, 35, 45, 50.
Detroit Edison Company, Detroit, Mich., 5, 27.
Detroit Testing Laboratories, Detroit, Mich., 40.
Dodge Bros., Detroit, Mich., 6, 27.
Draper Fund of the National Academy of Sciences, 43.
Du Pont de Nemours and Company, Wilmington, Delaware, 6.

EASTMAN KODAK COMPANY, Rochester, N.Y., 7, 52.
Edison, T. A., 17.
Edison Electric Lamp Works, Harrison, N.J., 13.
Edison Laboratories, East Orange, N.J., 17.
Electrical Testing Laboratories, New York, N.Y., 39.
Elizabeth Thompson Science Fund, 43.
Endowments for Scientific Research, 43.
Engineering, chemical, scheme for training in, 41.
Engineering Endowment Fund, 43.
Engineering Experiment Stations at Universities, 24, 26-29.
Expenditure, annual, of Manufacturing Corporations on research, 2.

FERMENTOLOGY, Wahl-Henius Institute of, 42.
Fitzgerald Laboratories, Inc., Niagara Falls, N.Y., 40.
Forest Products Laboratory of the Department of Agriculture, 28, 31, 36.
Franklin Institute, suggested co-operation of, in encouragement of research, 45.

GENERAL BAKELITE COMPANY, 19.
General Chemical Company, 19.
General Cotton Manufacturers' Association, 33.
General Electric Company, Schenectady, N.Y., 8, 13.
General Motors Company, Detroit, Mich., 10.
General Research Fund of the American Association for the Advancement of Science, 43.
Goodyear Tire and Rubber Company, Akron, O., 19.
Gypsum Industries Association, 20, 33.

HARDWOOD LUMBER ASSOCIATION, 20.
Harvard University, Cambridge, Mass., 24.

Hodgkins Fund (Smithsonian Institution), 43.
Hollow Tile Manufacturers' Association, 20, 33.

ILLINOIS CENTRAL RAILWAY, co-operation in research with University, 25.
Illinois State University, Urbana, Ill., 24, 50.
Imperial Research Laboratory, suggested centralised, 54.
Imperial Research, suggested organisation for, 51.
Industrial Laboratories. See Research Laboratories, industrial.
Industrial Research, British, organisation of, 50-55.
Industrial Research, definition of, 1.
Industrial Research, difference between pure science research and, 1.
Industrial Research. See also Research.
Industry, importance of research in pure science to, 1, 3, 9, 19, 46, 47, 49, 50, 51, 55.
Institute, Commonwealth, of Science and Industry, 51.
Institute of Industrial Research, Washington, D.C., 39.
International Acheson Graphite Company, Niagara Falls, N.Y., 11.
Iowa State College, Ames, Iowa, 26.

KANSAS, UNIVERSITY OF, Lawrence, Kan., 26.
Kennelly, Dr. A. E., letter re research, 45.

LABORATORIES, RESEARCH. See Research Laboratories.
Land Grant College Engineering Association, promotion of research legislation by, 44.
Land Grant Colleges, 21, 28, 44.
Lehigh University, South Bethlehem, Pa., 27.
Libraries, Research, of manufacturing corporations, 8, 9, 12.
Library, proposed Research, at Columbia University, 23.
Little, A. D., Laboratory of, Boston, Mass., 41.

MANUFACTURERS, assistance given to, 27-29, 33, 36, 39-42; attitude of British, to research, 48, 51, 56.
Manufacturers' Associations, research work of, 2, 20-21, 33.
Manufacturing Corporations, annual expenditure of, on research, 2; laboratories of, 2-20.
Manufacturing Plant in Laboratories, 5, 7, 8, 9, 11, 12, 13, 14, 16, 17, 19, 21, 30.

Marine Architecture, testing tank for, 27.
Massachusetts Institute of Technology, 24, 41, 42.
Master Car Builders' Association, 15.
Mechanic Arts Experiment Stations, suggested, 44, 45.
Mees, Dr. C. E. K., paper by, 45.
Mellon Institute of Industrial Research and School of Specific Industries, 2, 29-31, 46.
Michigan, University of, Ann Arbor, Mich., 6, 27.
Mines, Bureau of, 6, 31, 37, 45.
Morrell Act, 21.

NATIONAL ACADEMY OF SCIENCES, 43, 44.
National Association of Paint Manufacturers, 20.
National Association of Refrigeration, 20.
National Brick Manufacturers' Association, 20, 33.
National Canners' Association, 20.
National Carbon Company, Cleveland, O.,
National Cash Register Company, Dayton 11-12.
National Dairy Union, 20, 33.
National Electric Lamp Association, Cleveland, O., 13.
National Electric Light Association, 33.
National Institutions, research work in, 2, 31-38.
National Lime Manufacturers' Association, 20, 33.
National Physical Laboratory [British], 54, 55.
National Radium Institute, 38.
National Research Council, 44.
Nationalisation of Research in the United States, 44; in Great Britain, 51.
Naval Advisory Board, 45.
Nela Research Laboratory, 13.
New Jersey Zinc Company, New York, N.Y., 14.
Newlands Bill (for Mechanic Arts Experimentation), 44.

OHIO STATE UNIVERSITY, Columbus, Ohio, 28.
Organisation of British Industrial Research, 50-55.

PALMER PHYSICAL LABORATORY, Princeton University, 28.
Pennsylvania Railroad Company, Altoona, Pa., 15, 33, 43.
Pittsburg Plate Glass Company, Creighton, Pa., 19.
Pittsburg Testing Laboratory, Pittsburg, Pa., 40.
Pittsburg University, 29, 38.

Pittsfield Works (General Electric Company), 10.
Princeton University, N.J., 28.
Public Service, Research applied to, 4.
Purdue University, 29.
Pure Science Research, importance of, to industry, 1, 3, 9, 19, 46, 47, 49, 50, 51, 55; suggested nationalisation of, in Great Britain, 51.

RADIUM INSTITUTE, NATIONAL, 38.
Raymond Cement Pile Company, 29.
Reo Motor Company, Lansing, Mich., 16.
Research :—
application of, to manufacturing difficulties, 2, 4, 12; to public service, 4.
attitude of British manufacturers to, 48, 51, 56.
collection and distribution of results of, 5, 13, 23, 25, 29, 34, 36-39, 43, 44, 45, 49, 50, 55.
co-operation of scientific societies in, 2, 42-43.
co-ordination of, in the United States, 44-46.
cost of, in national institutions, 32, 36, 38.
definition of industrial, 1.
difference between pure science research and industrial, 1.
educational value of, 50, 53.
effect of home and export trade on, 44, 48, 49.
examples of, 5-42.
fellowships, establishment of, 27-29.
financial aspect of, 50, 52, 56.
for customers, 5, 13, 19, 21.
for establishing standard methods of testing and standard specifications, 4.
for specific new commercial objects, 3.
in industrial laboratories, striking features of, 19.
in pure science, importance of, to industry, 1, 3, 9, 19, 46, 47, 49, 50, 51, 55; suggested nationalisation of, in Great Britain, 51.
in relation to industrial conditions after the war, 52.
in universities and colleges, 2, 21-31; by staff, 22; centralisation of, 53, cost of, 23, 25, 27, 30; for private firms, 22; in experiment stations, 22.
nationalisation of, in the United States, 44.
necessity of public support for, 50, 56.
organisation of British industrial, 50-55.
overlapping in, 44, 52.
publication of results of, 5, 6, 8, 9, 12, 14, 16, 18, 19, 22, 25, 27, 29, 31, 34-39, 41-43, 50, 55.
scientific, endowments for, 43.
suggested organisation for imperial, 51.

Research Laboratories, Industrial:—
  classification of, 2; commercial, 2, 39-42; cost of erection and maintenance of, 7, 8, 15, 16, 18, 21, 41; examples of, 4-20; for individual works, 52; for groups of works, 53; manufacturing plant in, 5, 7, 8, 9, 11, 12, 13, 14, 16, 17, 19, 21, 30; profits from 3, 6, 9, 52; report relating to, 45; striking features of research work of, 19.
Research Laboratory, imperial centralised, 54.
Research Laboratory and Library, proposed, at Columbia University, 23.
Research Libraries of Manufacturing Corporations, 8, 9, 12.
Research Men, selection and training of, 31, 46, 47, 56; utilisation of, 47; value of, 49.
Rumford Fund of the American Academy of Arts and Sciences, 43.

SALARIES IN RESEARCH LABORATORIES, 30, 47.
Scientific Research, Endowments for, 43.
————— ————— See also Research.
Scientific Societies, co-operation of, in research, 2, 42-43.
Selection of Research Men, 31, 46, 47.
Sheffield district, central laboratory for research work in, 53.
Sibley College of Mechanical Engineering, 23.
Smithsonian Institution, 31, 35, 43.
Society of Automobile Engineers, 42.
Staff in industrial laboratories, 5-19, 39-41: in national institutions, 34, 36; in university laboratories, 23, 24, 26, 30.
Standard methods of testing and specifications, research for establishing, 4.
Standards, Bureau of, 15, 20, 31, 32-34, 46, 47, 50.
Studebaker Corporation, Detroit and South Bend, Ind., 16.

T. A. EDISON LABORATORIES, East Orange, N.J., 17.
Testing by Bureau of Standards, 32-34.
Testing Laboratories, Detroit, 40.
Testing Laboratories, Electrical, New York, 39.
Testing Laboratory, Pittsburg, 40.
Training of Research Men, 31, 46. 47, 56.

UNDERWRITERS' LABORATORY, 33.
United Gas Improvements Company, 19.
United Engineering Society, 42.
United States Rubber Company, New York, 19.
United States Steel Corporation, 19.
Universities and Colleges, research work of, 2, 21-31.
Universities, centralisation of research in colleges and, 53.
Universities, individual:—Clark, 22; Columbia, 23; Cornell, 23, 29, 38; Harvard, 24; Illinois, 24, 50; Kansas, 26; Lehigh, 27; Michigan, 6, 27; Ohio, 28; Pittsburg, 29, 38; Princeton, 28; Purdue, 29; Wisconsin, 28, 36; Yale, 28, 29.
University Professors in an industrial laboratory, 14.

WAHL-HENIUS INSTITUTE OF FERMENTOLOGY, Chicago, 42.
Warren Fund of the American Academy of Arts and Sciences, 43.
Western Electric Company, New York, N.Y., 18.
Westinghouse Electric and Manufacturing Company, East Pittsburg, Pa., 17.
Wisconsin, University of, 28, 36.
Wolcott Fund of the National Academy of Sciences, 43.
Worcester Polytechnic Institute, Worcester, Mass., 28, 29, 46.

YALE UNIVERSITY, 28, 29.

LONDON:
PUBLISHED BY HIS MAJESTY'S STATIONERY OFFICE.

To be purchased through any Bookseller or directly from
H.M. STATIONERY OFFICE at the following addresses:
IMPERIAL HOUSE, KINGSWAY, LONDON, W.C.2, and 28, ABINGDON STREET, LONDON, S.W.1;
37, PETER STREET, MANCHESTER; 1, ST. ANDREW'S CRESCENT, CARDIFF;
23, FORTH STREET, EDINBURGH;
or from E. PONSONBY, LTD., 116, GRAFTON STREET, DUBLIN;
or from the Agencies in the British Colonies and Dependencies,
the United States of America and other Foreign Countries of
T. FISHER UNWIN, LTD., LONDON, W.C.2.

Printed under the authority of His Majesty's Stationery Office,
By EYRE and SPOTTISWOODE, LTD., East Harding Street, E.C.4,
Printers to the King's most Excellent Majesty.

1917.

TECHNOLOGY AND SOCIETY

An Arno Press Collection

Ardrey, R[obert] L. **American Agricultural Implements.** In two parts. 1894

Arnold, Horace Lucien and Fay Leone Faurote. **Ford Methods and the Ford Shops.** 1915

Baron, Stanley [Wade]. **Brewed in America:** A History of Beer and Ale in the United States. 1962

Bathe, Greville and Dorothy. **Oliver Evans:** A Chronicle of Early American Engineering. 1935

Bendure, Zelma and Gladys Pfeiffer. **America's Fabrics:** Origin and History, Manufacture, Characteristics and Uses. 1946

Bichowsky, F. Russell. **Industrial Research.** 1942

Bigelow, Jacob. **The Useful Arts:** Considered in Connexion with the Applications of Science. 1840. Two volumes in one

Birkmire, William H. **Skeleton Construction in Buildings.** 1894

Boyd, T[homas] A[lvin]. **Professional Amateur:** The Biography of Charles Franklin Kettering. 1957

Bright, Arthur A[aron], Jr. **The Electric-Lamp Industry:** Technological Change and Economic Development from 1800 to 1947. 1949

Bruce, Alfred and Harold Sandbank. **The History of Prefabrication.** 1943

Carr, Charles C[arl]. **Alcoa, An American Enterprise.** 1952

Cooley, Mortimer E. **Scientific Blacksmith.** 1947

Davis, Charles Thomas. **The Manufacture of Paper.** 1886

Deane, Samuel. **The New-England Farmer,** or Georgical Dictionary. 1822

Dyer, Henry. **The Evolution of Industry.** 1895

Epstein, Ralph C. **The Automobile Industry:** Its Economic and Commercial Development. 1928

Ericsson, Henry. **Sixty Years a Builder:** The Autobiography of Henry Ericsson. 1942

Evans, Oliver. **The Young Mill-Wright and Miller's Guide.** 1850

Ewbank, Thomas. **A Descriptive and Historical Account of Hydraulic and Other Machines for Raising Water,** Ancient and Modern. 1842

Field, Henry M. **The Story of the Atlantic Telegraph.** 1893

Fleming, A. P. M. **Industrial Research in the United States of America.** 1917

Van Gelder, Arthur Pine and Hugo Schlatter. **History of the Explosives Industry in America.** 1927

Hall, Courtney Robert. **History of American Industrial Science.** 1954

Hungerford, Edward. **The Story of Public Utilities.** 1928

Hungerford, Edward. **The Story of the Baltimore and Ohio Railroad, 1827-1927.** 1928

Husband, Joseph. **The Story of the Pullman Car.** 1917

Ingels, Margaret. **Willis Haviland Carrier, Father of Air Conditioning.** 1952

Kingsbury, J[ohn] E. **The Telephone and Telephone Exchanges:** Their Invention and Development. 1915

Labatut, Jean and Wheaton J. Lane, eds. **Highways in Our National Life:** A Symposium. 1950

Lathrop, William G[ilbert]. **The Brass Industry in the United States.** 1926

Lesley, Robert W., John B. Lober and George S. Bartlett. **History of the Portland Cement Industry in the United States.** 1924

Marcosson, Isaac F. **Wherever Men Trade:** The Romance of the Cash Register. 1945

Miles, Henry A[dolphus]. **Lowell, As It Was, and As It Is.** 1845

Morison, George S. **The New Epoch:** As Developed by the Manufacture of Power. 1903

Olmsted, Denison. **Memoir of Eli Whitney, Esq.** 1846

Passer, Harold C. **The Electrical Manufacturers, 1875-1900.** 1953

Prescott, George B[artlett] **Bell's Electric Speaking Telephone.** 1884

Prout, Henry G. **A Life of George Westinghouse.** 1921

Randall, Frank A. **History of the Development of Building Construction in Chicago.** 1949

Riley, John J. **A History of the American Soft Drink Industry:** Bottled Carbonated Beverages, 1807-1957. 1958

Salem, F[rederick] W[illiam]. **Beer, Its History and Its Economic Value as a National Beverage.** 1880

Smith, Edgar F. **Chemistry in America.** 1914

Steinman, D[avid] B[arnard]. **The Builders of the Bridge:** The Story of John Roebling and His Son. 1950

Taylor, F[rank] Sherwood. **A History of Industrial Chemistry.** 1957

Technological Trends and National Policy, Including the Social Implications of New Inventions. Report of the Subcommittee on Technology to the National Resources Committee. 1937

Thompson, John S. **History of Composing Machines.** 1904

Thompson, Robert Luther. **Wiring a Continent:** The History of the Telegraph Industry in the United States, 1832-1866. 1947

Tilley, Nannie May. **The Bright-Tobacco Industry, 1860-1929.** 1948

Tooker, Elva. **Nathan Trotter:** Philadelphia Merchant, 1787-1853. 1955

Turck, J. A. V. **Origin of Modern Calculating Machines.** 1921

Tyler, David Budlong. **Steam Conquers the Atlantic.** 1939

Wheeler, Gervase. **Homes for the People,** In Suburb and Country. 1855

T
176
F48
1972

JUN 21 1973